DEVON AND CORNWALL RECORD SOCIETY

New Series, Volume 48

DEVON AND CORNWALL RECORD SOCIETY

New Series, Volume 48

KILLERTON, CAMBORNE AND WESTMINSTER

The Political Correspondence of Sir Francis and Lady Acland, 1910–29

Edited by

Garry Tregidga

Exeter

2006

© Devon and Cornwall Record Society,
Garry Tregidga 2006

ISBN 0 901853 48 8

Designed and typeset by Mike Dobson, Quince Typesetting
Sabon 10/12.5

Printed and bound in Great Britain
by Short Run Press Ltd, Exeter

Contents

Preface and Acknowledgements

This book reflects my interest for a number of years in the neglected story of Francis and Eleanor Acland. There is a tendency to remember either the achievements of previous generations of the family or the subsequent attempt of Sir Richard, their eldest son, to transform British politics during the Second World War through his creation of Common Wealth. This edited collection of the political correspondence of the family in the early decades of the twentieth century seeks to redress the balance. For the pre-war period it highlights the important contribution of both Francis and Eleanor to the campaign for female suffrage. In the aftermath of the First World War the Aclands then launched their own attempt to create a new centre-left force in British politics. By the late 1920s they were part of Lloyd George's inner circle when he made his final attempt to restore the declining fortunes of the Liberal party. Yet this is also a story of the political diversity of provincial Britain. Part of the appeal in approaching the Acland project was the way in which the core collection of letters in the Devon Record Office, supplemented by a combination of public and private correspondence from other archive centres and libraries, offered further insight into the peripheral world of constituency politics and regional distinctiveness. The letters are therefore interpreted from the contrasting perspectives of high and low politics during a crucial period of realignment.

I am indebted to a wide range of individuals and institutions for their support for the Acland project. It was Nicholas Orme, a past chairman of the Council of the Devon and Cornwall Record Society, who originally suggested the idea of producing an edited volume based on the papers in the Devon Record Office when I was completing my PhD. The subsequent publication of the book was assisted by a generous donation from the Wide family in memory of the late Stanley Maunder Wide who sadly died in 2003. He was a member of the Devon and Cornwall Record Society for many years and was passionately interested in Devon records, which he used for his own local history research. The support of the Acland family in allowing publication of the letters should also be noted. Sir John Acland, a past president of the Devon and Cornwall Record Society and a grandson of Francis and Eleanor, took a keen interest in the project from an early stage. Useful advice was later given by Sir John's son, Dominic, during my search for a cover photograph.

The majority of letters reproduced in this volume are preserved for future generations in the Devon Record Office. I am very grateful to John Draisey and his staff for advice and support during my many visits to the archive in Exeter. It should be noted at this stage that an abbreviated version of the DRO reference number has been used in order to avoid unnecessary repetition. For permission to consult other papers relating to either Francis or Eleanor Acland I am indebted to the staff of the Bodleian Library at Oxford, the Special Collections Department of the University of Bristol Library and the National Archives at Kew. My thanks also go to Pauline Quickfall at Liskeard Liberal Democrat Office for her kindness and assistance when studying the C.A. Millman papers and other non-catalogued material relating to the former Bodmin Liberal Association. Additional information, particularly in relation to the primary source material used in the extended introduction, came from a variety of resource centres. I would especially like to acknowledge the friendly and enthusiastic support of Terry Knight and his staff at Kresenn Kernow/Cornwall Centre in Redruth and Angela Broome at the Courtney Library, Royal Institution of Cornwall in Truro. I am similarly grateful to Denise Melhuish and Jeremy Pearson of the National Trust at Killerton for allowing me to reproduce the Acland family photograph displayed on the front cover.

Other individuals should be acknowledged for their part in the completion of this study. My thanks go to Treve Crago, a former colleague now living in Brittany, who originally pointed out the existence of the J.F. Williams correspondence with Francis, which he discovered as a result of his earlier investigation into the bitter events of the 1913 China Clay strike. Although the research for the book has been principally based on the use of written sources, notably letters, election addresses and newspapers, I would also like to thank George Pawley White for providing a unique 'living link' to the past through his personal recollections of Sir Francis during the time when he was MP for North Cornwall in the 1930s. At the Institute of Cornish Studies, I am very grateful to my colleagues, Bernard Deacon, Kayleigh Milden, Mandy Morris, Philip Payton and Sharron Schwartz, for their advice and assistance in recent years. Further encouragement and inspiration during the course of the project came from Sarah Austin, Laura Cripps, Monica Emerich, Bob Keys, Alistair and Susan Laming-Le Tissier, and Ron Perry. My parents, Stanley and Elisa Tregidga, have always encouraged me in my academic research and I am deeply grateful for their love and support.

Finally, I would like to thank Andrew Thorpe, the Honorary Editor of the Devon and Cornwall Record Society, for his enthusiasm and patience both throughout the course of this project and at the time of his earlier role in the 1990s as my PhD supervisor at the University of Exeter.

Garry Tregidga,
Penwithick,
Cornwall

Introduction

The years immediately before and after the First World War witnessed a dramatic realignment in British politics. In December 1910 the Liberals could still claim to be the natural party of government after winning three election victories in a row.[1] Just eight years later the party was struggling to survive as an independent and relevant force both at Westminster and in the country as a whole. Divided between the rival camps of Herbert Asquith and David Lloyd George the political heirs of Gladstone seemed increasingly unable to portray Liberalism as a credible movement for the twentieth century. In the first place the despairing supporters of Asquith, Liberal Prime Minister from 1908 until his resignation in December 1916, had fallen to fourth place in the House of Commons as a result of the 1918 election. On a superficial basis the position of the Coalition Liberals seemed far stronger as a result of Lloyd George's landslide victory. Yet the collapse of their coalition with the Conservatives in 1922, combined with the seemingly inevitable rise of Labour in the industrial regions of Britain, undermined the position of the Lloyd George group. Although the Liberals experienced a short-lived reunion and revival at the 1923 general election, the further polarisation of British politics in response to the first minority Labour government led to the party being firmly relegated to third place in 1924 with just forty seats in the House of Commons. Despite much effort thereafter, notably at the 1929 election, the Liberals were never able to escape their third-party status, and by the 1950s seemed to many to be on the verge of extinction. Much has been written since the late 1960s about this rapid transition from dominance to despair in the fortunes of the Liberal party. One view is that Liberalism was already losing ground to Labour in its industrial strongholds before 1914.[2] Other historians, such as Trevor Wilson and Duncan Tanner, have emphasised the political and

---

[1.] After January 1910 the Liberals were dependent on Irish Nationalist and Labour support in order to remain in office.

[2.] H. Pelling, *Popular Politics and Society in Late Victorian Britain*, London, 1968; K. Laybourn and J. Reynolds, *Liberalism and the rise of Labour, 1890–1918*, London, 1984; K. Laybourn, *The Rise of Labour: The British Labour Party, 1890–1979*, London, 1988.

social consequences of the First World War, while Chris Cook pointed out that the Liberal party actually remained a serious contender for government until its disastrous performance in 1924.[3]

These wider events and debates in British political history provide the context for assessing the correspondence of Francis Acland (1874–1939) and his wife Eleanor (1879–1933). In the first place it should be noted that Francis's political career as a Liberal candidate led him to contest a variety of constituencies throughout Britain during this period. Although initially elected for the Yorkshire division of Richmond in 1906, he had moved to Camborne by the time of the second election of 1910. In the early 1920s he served briefly as the Member for Tiverton before an unsuccessful attempt to win the Northumberland constituency of Hexham in 1929. Just three years later he returned to the House of Commons as a result of a by-election victory at North Cornwall and then held this seat until his death in 1939. The greater part of the letters in this collection cover the critical period of transition from December 1910 to November 1922 when Francis served as the Member of Parliament for the Cornish constituency of Camborne. This micro dimension is important for understanding the process of political realignment at the provincial level. Rather than focusing purely on the macro evidence of political change and continuity, a number of local and regional studies have been produced that consider the rise of Labour, the consolidation of the Conservatives and the decline of the Liberals in the provinces.[4] The Acland letters are important in this respect since they offer a local case study of the wartime challenge of Labour in what was formerly a key industrial stronghold of Liberalism. At the beginning of the period electioneering in Camborne, popularly known as the 'Mining Division', was still based on the traditional struggle between the old Liberal and Unionist parties. By 1917, however, Francis's letters to his wife were highlighting the local threat to Liberalism posed by the cultural and political power of the Labour movement. The nature of provincial politics also needs to be considered in relation to notions of

[3] T. Wilson, *The Downfall of the Liberal Party, 1914–1935,* London, 1966; D. Tanner, *Political Change and the Labour Party 1900–1918,* Cambridge, 1990; C. Cook, *The Age of Alignment: Electoral Politics in Britain, 1922–1929,* Macmillan, London, 1975; for a discussion of this period see G.R. Searle, *The Liberal Party: Triumph and Disintegration, 1886–1929,* London, 1992.

[4] For examples of regional and local political studies see D. Clark, *Colne Valley: Radicalism to Socialism,* London, 1981; P. Wyncoll, *The Nottingham Labour Movement, 1880–1940,* London, 1985; G. Tregidga, *The Liberal Party in South-West Britain since 1918: Political Decline, Dormancy and Rebirth,* University of Exeter Press, 2000. P. Payton, *The Making of Modern Cornwall: Historical Experience and the Persistence of 'Difference',* Redruth, 1992, demonstrates the need to consider issues of political realignment in Celtic Britain in the wider context of centre-periphery studies.

constituency representation and community identity. From this perspective the public and private reflections of the Aclands offer a unique insight into such topics as the constituency role of a Member of Parliament, the development of anti-metropolitanism and perceptions of ethnic and regional identity in the opening decades of the twentieth century.

Yet these years also represented the highpoint of Francis's political career at Westminster. He joined Herbert Asquith's Liberal government in April 1908 as a junior minister at the War Office and in October 1911 became Under Secretary of State at the Foreign Office. By January 1915 he seemed destined for high office when Asquith appointed him as Financial Secretary to the Treasury, the most senior non-cabinet post in the government. Although the formation of the first wartime coalition administration in May 1915 necessitated a move to the junior post of Parliamentary Secretary to the Board of Agriculture and Fisheries, the fact that Lord Selborne, the cabinet minister, was in the House of Lords meant that Francis had to represent the government in the Commons and became a member of the Privy Council.[5] In 1918, with many leading independent Liberals defeated in the general election, he emerged as a potential chairman of the parliamentary party and a leading advocate of a rejuvenated Liberal-Labour alliance. During the late 1920s he played an important role in attempts to revive the Liberal cause, notably in relation to the development of the party's land reform programme. Eleanor's contribution to Liberal party politics should also be recognised. She was one of the leading figures behind the creation of the pre-war Liberal Women's Suffrage Union and at the time of the 1929 election played a high-profile role as president of the Women's National Liberal Federation.[6] This means that the observations outlined in the political correspondence of the Aclands cover a variety of subjects including the campaign for female suffrage, Irish Home Rule, wartime politics and the Asquith-Lloyd George split. Both Francis and Eleanor corresponded with some of the leading figures in British politics and their letters reflect the changes taking place at the centre. In that sense the underlying appeal and importance of the Acland letters is the way in which the collection reflects the concerns of both high and low politics. Any interpretation of this material must therefore recognise the tensions that this sometimes caused for Francis Acland given his dual role both as the parliamentary representative of a remote constituency and as a junior government minister building a career in British politics.

[5.] Acland Papers, Devon Record Office, 1148 M 14/26, Herbert Asquith to Francis Acland, 28 May 1915.

[6.] For details of Lady Eleanor Acland's involvement with the Women's National Liberal Federation see *The Liberal Women's News*, November 1925.

It should be noted that the letters of Francis and Eleanor are drawn from a variety of sources. The greater part of the collection comes from the Acland family papers deposited at the Devon Record Office. Many of the letters written by Francis were intended to keep his wife informed of wider political developments at Westminster. This includes his personal reflections on ministerial changes during Asquith's last peacetime administration and the future of the Liberal party after the First World War. Other examples were written during his election campaign visits to Camborne in 1910 and again during his wartime visits to Cornwall in preparation for the 1918 general election. Eleanor herself was responsible for some of the letters, particularly to her eldest son Richard Thomas Dyke Acland (1906–90), and these examples outline her views on the state of British politics in the 1920s. The Devon Record Office collection also contains some correspondence with leading politicians like Asquith, Sir Edward Grey and Charles Trevelyan. Yet in order to present a complete picture of the period additional letters and election addresses have been included from the Asquith papers at the Bodleian Library in Oxford, the National Liberal Club collection at the University of Bristol, the Public Record Office in London and the South East Cornwall Liberal Democrat Office in Liskeard. A series of public letters to local newspapers and magazines adds another dimension to this edited collection. In some cases the correspondence was directly with the editors of local newspapers such as the *West Briton, Cornish Post,* and the *Cornubian.* On other occasions, however, Francis communicated initially with leading members of the Camborne Liberal Association and then requested that they disseminate his views to a wider audience through the press. This policy highlights his own perceptions on responsibilities and duties as a Member of Parliament. One might add that the occasional contradictions between his public and private correspondence, notably in relation to his views on post-war boundary changes in Cornwall, also provide a greater insight into the character of Francis and the history of the period as a whole.

This introduction to the letters will therefore consider events within the context of developments both at Westminster and in the provinces. The first section outlines the parliamentary traditions of the Acland family along with Francis's determination to maintain and enhance that legacy. Consideration is given to his successful election campaign in Camborne in December 1910 and his subsequent career as a junior minister under Asquith. This chronological overview then continues with a discussion of inter-war Liberalism from the personal perspective of the Aclands, notably in relation to the party's last determined challenge under the leadership of Lloyd George in the late 1920s and the wilderness years of the 1930s. The remaining sections then focus on the key political themes contained in the letters during the critical period from 1910 to 1929. Labour's challenge in industrial seats, combined with a growing sense of despair at the apparently imminent demise of Liberalism, figures prominently in the correspondence of Francis and Eleanor from the First World War onwards. Changing notions on dealing with this situation, not least through the advocacy of a more meaningful post-war relationship between the Liberal and Labour parties, offers further insight into the history of progressive politics. The final section of the introduction then considers events from a provincial perspective. Regional variations, ranging from anti-metropolitan concerns in Celtic Britain to agricultural discontent in rural Britain, ensured that political realignment was a complex process. An opportunity certainly existed for the Liberals to adopt a new anti-metropolitan role in response to the new political order at Westminster. The section concludes by looking at the reasons why the party enjoyed only limited success in reinventing itself in this way after the First World War.

The Acland Legacy

Francis Dyke Acland was born in Oxfordshire on 7 March 1874. He was the eldest son of Arthur Herbert Dyke Acland (1847-1926), originally from Killerton in the East Devon parish of Broadclyst, and Alice 'Elsie' Cunningham, the daughter of an Anglican clergyman at Witney.[7] Family tradition played an important part in the life and career of Francis. According to W.G. Hoskins, the Aclands should be regarded as the 'oldest surviving landed family' in Devon.[8] Their background in this respect dates back to their early origins as minor landowners in North Devon in the early Middle Ages. Loyalty to the Royalist cause in the Civil War led in 1644 to a baronetcy for the Aclands and in 1680 Killerton House was established as the family's principal residence. Subsequent acquisitions of property meant that by the second half of the eighteenth century the Aclands had become one of the most prominent landowning families in the South West of Britain with extensive estates scattered throughout Devon, Somerset and Cornwall. For Arthur, however, life as an Anglican clergyman seemed inevitable since it was his elder brother, Charles Thomas Dyke Acland (1842–1919), who was the heir to both Killerton and the baronetcy. During the 1870s Arthur combined his divinity studies with a history lectureship at Keble College, Oxford but by 1880 he had rebelled against his father's wishes by resigning from the clergy. This was followed by a career as chief administrator of Christ Church and a growing involvement in the education work of the

---

[7.] A. Acland, *A Devon Family: The Story of the Aclands,* Phillimore, Chichester, 1981, p. 113.
[8.] *Ibid,* xv.

Co-operative Movement that remained an abiding interest up until his death.[9]

Yet from a relatively early age it was assumed that Francis would eventually inherit the family estates. His uncle Charles Acland did not have any children from his marriage to Gertrude Walrond in 1879 so this meant that Arthur and his son were his heirs. Francis received his early education at Rugby, Arthur's old school, and from public school he went to Balliol College, Oxford, where he studied Modern History. His father's influence was reflected in a growing interest in educational issues and following a year's tour around the world after graduating from Oxford he decided to study education at the University of Jena in Germany. In 1900 he was appointed as a junior examiner with South Kensington Education Department and three years later he became the assistant director for secondary education in the West Riding of Yorkshire.[10] This move to the North of England led in August 1905 to his marriage to Eleanor Cropper, who came from a prominent Westmorland family. Richard was born a year later and their first child was then followed by Arthur Geoffrey (1908–64), Cuthbert Henry (1910–79) and Ellen (1913–24). This period also witnessed a more active involvement in party politics when Francis was adopted as the Liberal prospective parliamentary candidate for Richmond. This seat was hardly ideal territory for any Liberal since the last time that the party was successful was back in 1885. The Liberals could at least rely on core groups like the local nonconformists and the lead miners of Swaledale.[11] Moreover, Francis demonstrated an early flair for political oratory and benefiting from his party's landslide victory throughout Britain in the 1906 general election he eventually won the seat from the Unionists by 108 votes. Ann Acland added that Francis and Eleanor now 'set out on their married life with a splendid optimism which matched the mood of the new government. Liberals everywhere felt as if they were at the start of a new golden age of democracy'.[12]

Family tradition figured prominently in Francis's decision to embark on a parliamentary career. Reflecting their status in landed society the Aclands were expected to play a prominent role in public life and had represented both county and borough constituencies in the South West since the 1600s. The family's Royalist sympathies back in the 1640s meant that their natural allegiance was to the Tory cause but in 1867 Sir Thomas Dyke Acland

9. *Ibid,* pp. 111, 116, 119 and 151.
10. *Royal Cornwall Gazette,* 24 November 1910; *The Cornubian,* 22 December 1910.
11. H. Pelling, *Social Geography of British Elections, 1885–1910,* Macmillan, London, p. 311.
12. Acland, *A Devon Family,* p. 143.

(1809–98), the grandfather of Francis, decided to switch his allegiance to the Liberal party following a long period of disenchantment with official Conservatism in relation to issues like protectionism and parliamentary reform.[13] Charles eventually joined him in the House of Commons, representing East Cornwall and then North-East Cornwall, and briefly serving as a junior minister in Gladstone's 1885 administration. Arthur's political career with the Liberals was even more distinguished. In 1885 he was elected for the first time as the member for Rotherham and seven years later he joined Gladstone's government as the first cabinet minister for Education.[14] Although Arthur resigned from the House of Commons in 1898 on the grounds of ill health, he apparently played a pivotal role in 1905 in persuading the leading Liberal Imperialists, Sir Edward Grey and Richard Haldane, to serve under Henry Campbell-Bannerman, thereby ensuring that the Liberals were able to contest the 1906 election as a united party.[15] Duty and responsibility were important factors in the attitude displayed towards parliamentary politics by the Acland family. Ann Acland remarked that Charles, in contrast perhaps to his brother, saw parliamentary service as a family obligation. She added that 'National politics were never much to his taste, but it was his duty to get into parliament as a Liberal'.[16] One might add that a similar attitude can be detected at times in the personal correspondence of Francis. In October 1917 when he was considering the possibility of standing down from the House of Commons he wrote to his wife stating that 'I possess, as you do, somehow such a very large amount of general competence that I don't think I should for long be without pretty useful & honourable work'.[17] Notwithstanding the genuine commitment of Francis to progressive causes like internationalism and social reform, the rather pompous tone of this extract highlights an underlying desire to be seen as pursuing a traditional role in the affairs of state that befitted his status in landed society.

That establishment role was much in evidence during the years after the 1906 Liberal landslide. In 1906 Francis was appointed as private secretary to Haldane at the War Office and two years later became the department's Financial Secretary. Yet Francis's career suffered a setback in January 1910 when he lost Richmond by 1,083 votes to the Unionists. By-election defeats

---

[13.] *Ibid,* pp. 6, 12, 88 and 99.
[14.] For further background information on the career of Arthur Acland see *Oxford Dictionary of National Biography,* Vol. 1, University of Oxford Press, 2004, pp. 148–51.
[15.] Acland, *A Devon Family,* pp. 141–43.
[16.] *Ibid,* p. 118.
[17.] Acland papers, 1148 M 14/681, Francis Acland to Eleanor Acland, 30 October 1917.

in the years leading up to the general election had indicated that the tide was turning for Liberalism. In the event Asquith was to emerge as leader of the largest single party in the House of Commons but he was dependent on votes from Labour and the Irish Nationalists in order to form a government. Francis was one of the losers on the Liberal side. Out of parliament he now had to wait to be selected for a safe Liberal seat. An opportunity arose when Albert Dunn, Liberal MP for Camborne since 1906, decided that he would not be defending his seat in the December 1910 election.[18] Camborne seemed a highly desirable seat for a radical like Francis. Although the seat had been briefly lost to a popular Liberal Unionist in 1895, there was a strong Liberal tradition based on the loyalty of the mining community and the numerical strength of Cornish Methodism.[19] Dunn had held the seat at the previous election with nearly two thirds of the vote and there was no serious challenge from the Labour party, which contrasted with the situation in a number of Liberal strongholds in industrial regions like the North of England. Francis was regarded as a rising star in national politics and on 26 November 1910 delegates of the Camborne Liberal association formally adopted him as candidate.[20]

The excitement of pre-war electioneering features prominently in Francis' account of his first contest at Camborne. Writing to Eleanor he explained that following the adoption meeting the Young Liberals had organised a torchlight procession through the streets of Camborne accompanied by singing, 'cheering and jolly good fellowing'. This enthusiasm continued throughout the election campaign with the 'red & blue', the traditional Liberal colours in the Mining Division, much in evidence.[21] However, his Unionist opponent, Dr George Coates, attempted to reduce the Liberal majority by shifting the focus of the election campaign away from the core election issue of the reform of the House of Lords to Cornish concerns over Irish Home Rule. Anti-Catholicism on the part of the Duchy's Methodist majority, combined with tensions in the United States between Cornish and Irish diaspora communities, meant that the policy of granting Home Rule to Ireland was not popular.[22] Following the Liberal split of 1886 it was the breakaway Liberal Unionists, who initially tended to be radical on domestic issues but conservative on imperial matters, that emerged as the

[18.] *West Briton,* 4 July 1910; *Royal Cornwall Gazette,* 24 November 1910.
[19.] Pelling, *Social Geography of British Elections,* p. 160 and 165.
[20.] Acland papers, 1148 M 14/512, Francis Acland to Eleanor Acland, 27 November 1910; *West Briton,* 22 December 1910; *The Cornubian,* 1 December 1910.
[21.] Acland papers, 1148 M 14/512, Francis Acland to Eleanor Acland, 27 November 1910; 1148 M 14/ 513, Francis Acland to Eleanor Acland, ? December 1910.
[22.] G. Tregidga, 'The Politics of the Celto-Cornish Revival, 1886–1939' in P. Payton (ed.), *Cornish Studies: Five,* University of Exeter Press, 1997, pp. 128–30.

dominant political force in Cornwall. They remained as the largest force at the parliamentary level until 1900 and it was not until 1906 that they lost their remaining strongholds with all seven seats going Liberal. However, after January 1910 the Liberal majority in the House of Commons was dependent on the votes of the Irish Nationalists and there was now an opportunity for the Unionists to exploit the traditional fear of Home Rule. Coates claimed that 'it would be an everlasting disgrace to the Noncon-formists here if they put in a man who voted in favour of . . . putting the Nonconformists in the North of Ireland under the heels of a majority ruled by the Catholic priests'.[23] Francis also found himself on the defensive because of his aristocratic background since Coates, a member of the medical profession, presented himself as a self-made man who 'was not a great landowner nor a large capitalist and . . . had no axe to grind. He had had to make his own living and he had earned everything he had now'.[24]

As the campaign developed Francis was increasingly uneasy about Liberal prospects in the neighbouring Cornish divisions. The election of December 1910 was the last contest in which voting took place for individual constituencies on separate days. Initial declarations were seen as influencing the trend in subsequent polls and Francis believed that the early loss of 'seats in the West ... will affect things here'.[25] The small borough of Falmouth & Penryn had already been lost at the previous election and in the December contest the Unionists emerged victorious in Bodmin. Francis explained that 'the truth must be that in the nonconformist districts where we would expect things to perk up because of the lessened Tory pressure and work, people have been so thoroughly worked up by religious bigotry against Home Rule'.[26] Nonetheless, the Liberals were still the dominant party in Cornwall after the election with five of the seven seats. Even Truro, which Francis thought was vulnerable to a strong challenge by the Unionists, was retained fairly comfortably. The margin of Francis's lead over Coates was 31.0 per cent and this meant that Camborne was the safest Liberal seat in the South West of Britain. At the declaration of the results Sir Arthur Carkeek, a leading local Liberal who had invited Francis to stay at his home during the course of the election campaign, described their new member as 'a man full of lofty ideals, high principles, straight in every walk of life, full of power and political sagacity who would go far in the counsels of the nation (cheers)'.[27]

[23.] *Royal Cornwall Gazette,* 1 and 8 December 1910.
[24.] *Ibid.*
[25.] Acland papers, 1148 M 14/514, Francis Acland to Eleanor Acland, 13 December 1910.
[26.] *Ibid,* 1148 M 14/516, Francis Acland to Eleanor Acland, ? December 1910.
[27.] *West Briton,* 22 December 1910.

Table 1: Percentage election results for the Camborne constituency, 1900–10 [28]

	1900	1903[1]	1906	J.1910	D.1910
Liberal	50.9	55.4	65.0	66.0	65.5
Unionist	49.1	44.6	33.5	34.0	34.5
Other	–	–	1.5[2]	–	–
Turnout	76.0	74.2	77.2	81.2	71.9

[1.] A by-election was held on 8 April 1903.
[2.] The third candidate in 1906 stood for the Social Democratic Federation.

With a safe seat in the House of Commons Francis could now resume his ministerial career. On 30 January 1911 Asquith invited him to take his 'old place' at the War Office and later that same year he moved to the Foreign Office. However, Francis expressed to Eleanor his preference for an appointment to a domestic post, such as Education or Agriculture, and he regarded this new appointment as a setback.[29] His disappointment was understandable particularly since the years leading up to the First World War saw a continuing focus on important home issues like labour relations, which as the Acland letters indicate had significant implications for Cornwall as a result of the 1913 clay strike, and the campaign for female suffrage. In regard to the latter issue both Francis and Eleanor attempted to move their party towards reform. The Aclands found themselves in a difficult position in the pre-war period when confronted by the militant campaign of the female suffragettes on one hand and the divisions within the Liberal party on the other. Eleanor was vice-president of the South Western federation of the National Union of Women's Suffrage Societies (NUWSS) at this time. In 1914 she announced her resignation on the grounds that the NUWSS was preventing committee members from actively supporting Liberal candidates. Seeking a practical course of action Eleanor emerged as a prominent member of the Liberal Women's Suffrage Union (LWSU) whose members were pledged to only campaign for those Liberal candidates who supported votes for women.[30] Similarly, Francis pursued a pro-active approach at Westminster by writing a memorandum to Asquith in favour of an extension of the franchise for both men and women on 'a broad

[28.] All election statistics used in this study are based on F.W.S. Craig, *British Parliamentary Election Results 1885–1918*, Chichester, 1974; F.W.S. Craig, *British Parliamentary Election Results 1918–49*, Chichester, 1983.
[29.] Acland papers, 1148 M 14/24, Herbert Asquith to Francis Acland, 30 January 1911; 1148 M 14/518, Francis Acland to Eleanor Acland, ? October 1911.
[30.] *The Liberal Woman's News*, November 1925, No. 48, pp. 109–10; *The Cornubian*, 2 July 1914. It is significant that Millicent Fawcett, the leader of the NUWSS, described the LWSU as 'Mrs Acland's society'. See J. Vellacott, *From Liberal to Labour with Women's Suffrage: The Story of Catherine Marshall*, McGill-Queen's University Press, 1993, p. 279.

democratic basis' and supporting a new Liberal Suffrage Society under the presidency of Grey.[31] Land reform was another major domestic concern in the pre-war period but in this case the contribution of the Aclands came from Francis's father after he was appointed as the chairman of the government's Land Inquiry Committee. The report produced by Arthur's committee in October 1913 was then adopted by Lloyd George, the Chancellor of the Exchequer, as the central plank of the government's domestic programme in preparation for the next general election.[32]

Yet the outbreak of war in August 1914 transformed the political scene. Not surprisingly many of the letters written at this time reflect Francis's wartime responsibilities as Grey's deputy at the Foreign Office. In a public letter to *The Cornubian* on 11 August he correctly predicted that the war would 'be a hideous, long, grim struggle – not a matter of weeks but of months, perhaps of years'. Even at this early stage he emphasised the overriding necessity 'to make it impossible that such a struggle should ever again be waged upon the earth'.[33] Yet in a letter to Eleanor nine days later he was slightly more optimistic about the prospects for a speedy resolution to events. The British Expeditionary Force had reached Maubeuge in line with a military timetable drawn up by the allies some three years earlier and Acland remarked that if the Germans were unable to break through into north-eastern France then 'the general belief is that they are done'. Perhaps echoing the sentiment of the time he even added 'I wish I were there rather'.[34] In reality the British were still unsure of how best to defend Belgian neutrality. Opinions varied as to whether the British Expeditionary Force should be sent to Antwerp, Amiens or on the left wing of the French forces at Maubeuge. On 6 August the cabinet had finally decided that British troops should be sent to Amiens. For A.J.P. Taylor, however, this particular event pointed to the powerlessness of the Liberal government with responses dictated solely by the military's rigid adherence to timetables. Taylor claimed that 'no one took any notice' of the cabinet's attempt to retain a freedom of manoeuvre for the British forces. 'The timetable said

---

[31.] Herbert Asquith papers, Bodleian Library, Oxford, MS. Asquith 13, fol. 89, Francis Acland to Eric Drummond, c. November 1912; Acland papers, 1148 M 14/523, Francis Acland to Eleanor Acland, undated (c. 1913). Vellacott, *From Liberal to Labour with Women's Suffrage,* highlights the importance of both Francis and Eleanor in the campaign for female suffrage. Francis, for example, was apparently regarded as the most sympathetic member of the government, pp. 267 and 279.

[32.] Acland, *A Devon Family,* p. 146; I. Packer, *Lloyd George, Liberalism and the Land: The Land Issue and Party Politics in England, 1906–1914,* Woodbridge, suggests that Arthur Acland's role as chairman was more symbolic than practical given his ill health at this time (pp. 84–5).

[33.] *The Cornubian,* 6 and 13 August 1914.

[34.] Acland papers, 1148 M 14/616, Francis Acland to Eleanor Acland, 20 August 1914.

Maubeuge. To Maubeuge it went. In this accidental way Great Britain
found herself involved as a continental Power in a continental war'.[35]

In the early years of the war Francis seemed destined to finally enter the
cabinet. A series of minor promotions led in May 1915 to his appointment
as a Privy Councillor in order to represent the Board of Agriculture in the
House of Commons. Earlier in the year he had been regarded as a strong
candidate to replace Percy Illingworth as the Liberal party's Chief Whip,
and by August 1916 he was attempting to use his influence with Grey in
order to realise his earlier objective of following in his father's footsteps
by becoming the President of the Board of Education.[36] However, the
political crisis of December 1916 when Lloyd George replaced Asquith as
Prime Minister was to mark the end of Francis's eight years of service as a
government minister. Although offering to support the new administration
'in any possible way', he now went into the political wilderness with the
other anti-Coalition Liberals.[37] Yet Francis was increasingly concerned by
the failure of Asquith to mount a real challenge to the government. Writing
towards the end of 1917 he claimed that the former Prime Minister was
'too much of a gentleman to hit hard'. The party was also failing to develop
a post-war reconstruction programme and he was particularly critical of
the 'ex-Cabinet ministers [who] might have done more than they have
done in working out policies on social questions'. In these circumstances
Francis concluded that 'I really think the Liberal party is dead & that one
will simply have to think of men & policies after the war – not of parties'.[38]
Such comments tend to confirm the view that it was the events of the First
World War, notably the long-term impact of the Asquith-Lloyd George
split, which created a negative mindset amongst radical Liberals that the
party was now in a state of imminent demise.

Realignment was made possible through the existence of the Labour
party as an alternative vehicle for progressive politics. In May 1919 Charles
Trevelyan, a former junior minister who had moved from the Liberals to
Labour, informed Eleanor that in his view parties were 'only methods of
combining for political purposes'. Since the Liberals had now lost their
reputation for moral and intellectual leadership it was time for radicals

[35] A.J.P.Taylor (introduction by Chris Wrigley), *The First World War and its
Aftermath,* London, 1998.
[36] Acland papers, 1148 M 14/638, Francis Acland to Eleanor Acland, 16 August
1916. A revealing insight can be seen in S. Koss, *Asquith,* London, 1976, who
stated that Francis was 'disqualified' from becoming Liberal Chief Whip 'on
two counts: he had a suffragette wife, and he struck Asquith as "a rather angular
man"' (p. 176).
[37] *West Briton,* 11 and 21 December 1916.
[38] Acland papers, 1148 M 14/687, Francis Acland to Eleanor Acland, ? November
1917; 1148 M 14/698, Francis Acland to Eleanor Acland, ? December 1917.

and progressives to look elsewhere. He added that he did not 'expect much from the Labour party except that it will manage to evolve the organisation which will pretty soon get hold of the government, probably to make a horrid mess of it'. What was significant was that it offered 'a new conscience and policy' that contrasted markedly with the timidity of the Asquithian leadership.[39] Moreover, the general election of 1918 marked a significant turning point since the working class vote was now moving away from the Liberals. Only a small number of Independent Liberals were returned to the House of Commons[40] and Francis retained Camborne by the relatively narrow margin of 532 votes in a straight fight with Labour, which was an indication in itself of the changing nature of party politics at the provincial level. As will be discussed later, many of the letters written by Francis at this time reflect his growing disillusionment with both constituency affairs and parliamentary politics. Less than fourteen months after the election he announced his intention of standing down at the next election. In February 1920 in a letter to the Camborne Liberal Association he made no mention of any political factors but explained that this decision was due to 'reasons of health and the pressure of new and heavy responsibilities which have come upon me in the West of England since the last election'. Those 'heavy responsibilities' had resulted from the death of Charles in February 1919. Arthur had automatically inherited the Acland baronetcy but preferred to remain in London until his own death in 1926. It was left to Francis to take over the running of the Killerton estates and he had already settled in Devon before the death of his uncle in order to gain practical experience of estate management.[41]

Yet this decision did not mark the end of his political career. Rumours that Francis intended to contest Tiverton on the Devon-Somerset border had been circulating for some time before his eventual decision to withdraw from Camborne. Although the constituency covered the core Acland estates at Killerton, it was by nature a Conservative stronghold. Tory landowners dominated constituency politics and a Liberal had never represented this predominately rural seat since its creation in 1885.[42] The prospects for a Liberal victory had been further undermined in 1918 when a Labour candidate was able to poll a respectable vote and divide the anti-Conservative

---

[39.] Acland papers, 1148 M 14/889, Charles Trevelyan to Eleanor Acland, 24 May 1919.

[40.] Accounts of the number of Independent Liberals returned in 1918 vary widely from 14 to 36. This reflects the fact that many of the Liberals elected without a 'coupon' of support from the government still backed Lloyd George. See Cook, *Age of Alignment*, p. 7.

[41.] *Cornish Post*, 14 and 21 February 1920.

[42.] Pelling, *Social Geography of British Elections*, p. 172; *Express and Echo*, 17 November 1922.

vote in the process. Yet Francis welcomed the challenge of contesting Tiverton following his recent disillusionment with Westminster politics. His status as a prominent member of a local landed family meant that for once a Liberal could benefit from the politics of deference. Discontented farmers and agricultural labourers backed his challenge in the 1922 general election, which resulted in an impressive swing to the Liberals who were only 74 votes behind Weston Sparkes, the winning Conservative. An early opportunity to win Tiverton suddenly emerged in June 1923 following the death of Sparkes. The Conservatives were determined to counter the local popularity of the Aclands and they adopted Gilbert Acland-Troyte, a relative of Francis, as their candidate. Both parties fought a vigorous campaign with turnout in the constituency rising to nearly ninety per cent of the electorate, while the Labour vote, which had already started to move over to Francis in the preceding general election, basically collapsed. In the event Francis was returned to Westminster by the narrow margin of 403 votes. Only a few months later came the 1923 general election and yet another exciting contest at Tiverton with Francis again victorious albeit with an even smaller majority of just three votes.

The events at Tiverton fit into a wider pattern for the Liberals at this time. By 1923 the two wings of the Liberal party had briefly come together in response to the decision of Stanley Baldwin, the Conservative Prime Minister, to hold an early election on a protectionist platform. The Liberals, though still the third party in the House of Commons, demonstrated that they could still be a significant force in British politics by winning 158 seats compared to 191 for Labour and 258 for the Conservatives. Yet the party's gains tended to be at the expense of the Conservatives in the shire counties and cathedral cities rather than reversing Liberal losses to Labour in industrial and urban Britain. Francis's personal victory in Tiverton was echoed in other places like Worcester and Oxford that lacked a Liberal tradition.[43] It was perhaps only to be expected that the fragile foundations of the Liberal recovery were to be undermined by the events of 1924. With the Conservatives firmly established as the real alternative to James Ramsay MacDonald's first minority Labour administration the electorate was now forced to choose between what had become the two principal parties. In the general election of October 1924 the Liberals were forced on the defensive by a rejuvenated Conservative party that exploited the Liberal party's voting record in keeping Labour in office. The South West of Britain, which had been one of the main Liberal strongholds in 1923, now moved decisively to the Conservatives. Francis fought a spirited campaign based on his personal record in relation to measures like the 1924

[43.] For a discussion of the electoral performance of the Liberals in the early 1920s see Cook, *Age of Alignment*.

Agricultural Wages Board Act but his position was even more vulnerable than many of his colleagues and he eventually lost Tiverton by 1,659 votes.

Table 2: Percentage election results for the Tiverton constituency, 1918–24

	1918	1922	1923	1923	1924
Conservative	57.2	46.9	48.1	50.0	53.2
Liberal	28.7	46.5	49.9	50.0	46.8
Labour	14.1	6.6	2.0*	–	–
Turnout	64.8	80.1	88.1	87.4	90.2

* The official Labour nominee for Tiverton in 1922 contested the by-election in June 1923 as an Independent Labour candidate.

The defeat of Francis at Tiverton did not mark the end of his political career. In the late 1920s he played a pivotal role in attempts to rejuvenate the Liberal party in association with Lloyd George. This shift in allegiance might seem surprising given Acland's earlier support for Asquith but in the changing circumstances of the period he was attracted by his desire to remould Liberalism as a modern and progressive force. Following Asquith's elevation to the House of Lords the leadership of the party in the Commons had passed to Lloyd George who now set out to transform the staid image of Liberalism through a series of detailed policy reviews. A committee of experts that included the economist John Maynard Keynes produced the most famous of these reports entitled *Britain's Industrial Future,* the so-called *Yellow Book,* in 1928. The campaign version of this report emphasised the need for government planning in relation to the economy and Lloyd George's subsequent pledge to conquer unemployment was central to the party's national campaign in 1929. A radical policy review had long appealed to Francis who had criticised Asquith during the First World War for failing to develop a popular programme. In 1925 he was the leading political figure associated with Lloyd George's land policy, the *Green Book.* Echoing his father's role in the immediate pre-war period Francis's reputation as a progressive landowner meant that he now emerged as a key ally of Lloyd George. The new chairman of the Liberal parliamentary party even launched his land campaign at a mass rally at Killerton in September 1925 and Francis became his principal supporter for the policy through a series of articles and speeches.[44] However, critics within the party claimed that the new policy would lead to state control of agriculture and Lloyd George was forced to modify the proposals in order for them to be accepted at a special meeting of the National Liberal Federation in February 1926. The divisions caused particular embarrassment for Francis. Opposition from leading

[44.] For a review of the Killerton meeting see *Liberal Women's News,* November 1925, p. 112.

members of the executive committee of Tiverton Liberal Association meant that he was forced to resign as prospective parliamentary candidate in December 1925.[45]

Yet the hostility of Asquith's supporters meant that the Aclands became even more loyal to Lloyd George. Eleanor supported his sympathetic stance towards the miners during the 1926 General Strike unlike many other leading figures in the party and in the 1929 election she had a chance to campaign vigorously for the party's radical programme after becoming President of the Women's National Liberal Federation.[46] This election had marked the culmination of the Liberal revival of the late 1920s. With Lloyd George firmly in control of the party following the resignation of Asquith in October 1926 the scene was set for a final challenge to the other two parties. By-election successes, combined with lavish financial support from Lloyd George's political fund, meant that the party could enter the election in buoyant mood with 513 candidates. This included Francis who had been selected for Hexham in Northumberland and his son Richard who fought his first election at Torquay. Hexham had been a Liberal stronghold before the First World War and even in 1923 the party had won the seat.[47] Similarly, Torquay had been narrowly won in 1923 and was just the sort of seat the party needed to win in order to make a sustained breakthrough. Yet the election was to result in only a relatively small increase for the Liberals with just 59 seats compared to 260 for the Conservatives and 288 for Labour. The Liberal losers included Francis who had only succeeded in reducing the Conservative majority in Hexham. A crucial factor was a swing to Labour, which could count on the support of the coal miners in parts of the constituency, and a similar fate befell Richard.[48]

The defeat of Francis meant that he was unable to play an active role in the events that led up to the formation of the National government in 1931. Eleanor expressed the hope that we can 'trust the fortunate ones [returned in the election] to present a more united front than did the Liberal Party in the last parliament'.[49] Her high-profile role was extended in June 1931 when Lloyd George appointed her as the first female member

[45.] Tiverton Liberal Association papers, Devon Record Office, 4996 G/A1, executive committee minutes, 13 November 1925; special meetings, 18 December 1925 and 12 February 1926.
[46.] Acland papers, 1148 M/1086, Eleanor Acland to Richard Acland, 23 May 1926; *The Liberal Women's News,* April 1929, p. 223.
[47.] Pelling, *Social Geography of British Elections,* pp. 169–70 and 333.
[48.] The Conservative percentage lead in Hexham was reduced from 18.7 per cent in 1924 to 6.9 per cent in 1929. Richard did not even do so well as his father since the Conservative majority in Torquay was only reduced from 18.8 to 12.2 per cent.
[49.] *Liberal Women's News,* June 1929, p. 42.

of the Liberal Shadow Cabinet in her WNLF capacity.[50] However, the party soon reverted to the factional divisions of the recent past. Strategic differences over the parliamentary party's relationship to MacDonald's second minority Labour administration exacerbated underlying personal and ideological tensions at Westminster. The position of the Liberals was further complicated in August 1931 when the country's growing economic problems led MacDonald to form a National coalition ostensibly representing the three main parties. In the short term the new administration was regarded as the 'nearest approach to a Liberal government' since the war as it offered the party an opportunity to participate at cabinet level.[51] If Francis had won in 1929 it seems likely that he would have also returned to office at this time and as a former junior minister it is even possible that he might have finally realised his objective of entering the cabinet. The new administration proved to be only a temporary solution to the party's problems. In October 1931 it was agreed that the parties that formed the National government should appeal to the country for a so-called 'doctor's mandate' to introduce any measures, including tariffs, that would create economic prosperity. The Liberals, who had traditionally advocated free trade, now fought the election as three separate groups, with the Liberal Nationals closely allied to the Conservatives, the official Liberals led by Sir Herbert Samuel adopting a middle course and a smaller anti-government group supporting Lloyd George. Francis did not even stand as a candidate, preferring instead to give his support to Eleanor who obtained a respectable second place at Exeter and to Richard's narrowly unsuccessful challenge at Barnstaple.[52]

In the aftermath of the 1931 election the credibility of the Samuelite Liberals was further undermined by the protectionist agenda of the Conservative-dominated coalition. The introduction of a series of tariff measures resulted in the resignation of the Samuelite ministers in September 1932 and the official Liberals now moved to the government backbenches. Many Liberals, including Francis, preferred a complete separation but it was not until November 1933 that the party finally moved into opposition.[53] This

---

[50.] *Ibid,* June 1931, p. 606.

[51.] *Cornish Guardian,* 10 and 24 September 1931.

[52.] For a detailed study of this particular election see A. Thorpe, *The British General Election of 1931,* Oxford, 1991. Eleanor stood as a parliamentary candidate for the first and last time in this election. She came second at Exeter with 23.2 per cent in a seat that was rarely contested by the Liberals during the inter-war period. Richard benefited from the decision of the Labour party not to contest Barnstaple so that the Conservative lead only increased from 2.0 to 4.4 per cent.

[53.] C. Cook, *A Short History of the Liberal Party, 1900–84,* London, 1984, p. 118; *Cornish Guardian,* 4 May and 9 November 1933.

confusing period in Liberal history also saw the return of Francis to Westminster. In July 1932 he defended the Liberal seat of North Cornwall in a by-election that followed the death of Sir Donald Maclean. By the early 1930s the isolated and rural constituency of North Cornwall was regarded as the safest Liberal seat in the South West. The absence of a strong industrial base for Labour, combined with a tradition of radical nonconformity amongst the small farmers of the area, certainly gave an advantage to Liberalism. Nonetheless, it was indicative of the changing fortunes of the party that even a seat like North Cornwall was now vulnerable to a small swing to the Conservatives. In 1924 the Liberals had actually lost the seat for the first time in the party's history. Notwithstanding the victory of Maclean in 1929, the impact of in-migration in the coastal towns and villages of the constituency was seen as a long-term factor benefiting the Conservatives and it was generally expected that Francis would be defeated.[54] In the event, however, he retained North Cornwall with a slightly increased majority. Francis benefited from a local tradition of deference towards the Aclands. The family's estates in Cornwall were concentrated in the northern part of the constituency, while his uncle had been a respected member for the division in the late nineteenth century. Local respect for the Aclands was symbolic of a continuing 'acceptance of the Liberal faith' in the villages and hamlets of the area.[55] Francis was able to consolidate the support of the rural communities in the early 1930s by focusing on agricultural issues such as the radical reform of tithes and the creation of a new Agricultural Commission to encourage the dairy products of the South West. Moreover, the absence of a Labour candidate meant that 'large numbers of Labour voters' simply transferred their allegiance to the Liberals in order to prevent a Conservative victory.[56] By 1935 Francis had been able to forge a local anti-Conservative alliance with Labour in his constituency. He even attempted to extend this pact to neighbouring constituencies in association with A.L. Rowse, the Labour candidate for Penryn & Falmouth, and in the

---

[54.] David Lloyd George papers, House of Lords Record Office, H/33, newspaper cutting relating to the 1939 North Cornwall by-election; D. Dutton, *A History of the Liberal Party in the Twentieth Century,* Palgrave, 2004, p. 124.

[55.] *Cornish Guardian,* 14 July 1932; *Western Morning News,* 27 November 1935. K. Beswetherick, *The Aclands and Budehaven: the story of a Devon Family and a Cornish Town,* self publication, 1995, pp. 31 and 42, highlights the local deference shown towards Francis and Eleanor. In 1928 a local vicar remarked that 'as he went amongst the people of Bude he constantly saw photographs of the Acland family put in honoured places in the home because they represented the kindness and generosity which had been carried on in this place by that family' (p. 42).

[56.] *Cornish Guardian,* 30 June, 21 July and 28 July 1932; 21 November 1935.

general election of that year he was again returned for North Cornwall after another straight fight with the Conservatives.[57]

Table 3: Percentage election results for the North Cornwall constituency, 1923–35

	1923	1924	1929	1931	1932	1935
Liberal	56.5	46.4	49.7	49.1	52.4	51.3
Conservative	43.5	53.6	42.3	45.3	47.6	48.7
Labour	–	–	8.0	5.6	–	–
Turnout	75.6	78.0	86.1	85.7	80.8	79.9

By 1935, however, the electoral position of the Liberal party was even weaker than before. David Dutton's recent survey of this period concluded that Baldwin's 'version of Liberal Toryism had now captured the vital centre ground of British politics'.[58] Despite a modest improvement in the Liberal vote in some constituencies, which included Richard's victory for the first time at Barnstaple by the narrow margin of 464 votes, the party seemed in terminal decline with just 21 seats in the House of Commons. Francis, now regarded as the 'elder statesman of the tiny handful of Liberals who formed the parliamentary party', seemed to be contemplating retirement from Westminster at this time. He was seriously ill in October 1938 and three months later announced his intention of standing down from North Cornwall at the next general election, which was expected in 1939 or 1940.[59] Interestingly, he did not regard this decision as the end of his involvement in party politics since he had started to take an interest in the campaign for a Popular Front. By the late 1930s a growing belief that Labour would be unable to defeat the National Government in its own right led to calls for an alliance of the opposition parties. For many independent Liberals, whose party had previously been dismissed as an irrelevance, the prospect of a Popular Front offered an opportunity for political realignment. At the national level the campaign was hindered because of Labour suspicion of the movement's Communist origins. However, there was more potential with the localised version of a Front since constituency pacts to maximise the opposition vote would benefit the Liberals in seats where they were still the main challengers to the Conservatives.[60] The campaign received a major boost at the Bridgwater by-election in November 1938 when Vernon Bartlett, an Independent Progressive candidate supported by the local Liberal and Labour parties,

---

[57.] *Ibid*, 25 October 1934 and 29 October 1935.
[58.] Dutton, *History of the Liberal Party*, p. 136.
[59.] Acland, *A Devon Family*, p. 152; *West Briton*, 12 June 1939.
[60.] For a discussion of Popular Front politics see Tregidga, *Liberal Party in South-West Britain*, pp. 87–96.

captured the seat from the Conservatives. Francis had been advocating a progressive coalition since the First World War and he now described Bartlett's victory as a 'good example of what can be done if all working-class people, putting it broadly, will work together'.[61] Richard had played a pivotal role in arranging the electoral pact at Bridgwater and Francis now prepared to support Michael Pinney, a Liberal who had been selected to fight his old seat at Tiverton as an Independent Progressive.[62]

But this final political challenge was not to be. On 9 June 1939, aged just 65, he was found dead in his bed at Brook's Club in London following an acute attack of asthma. Eleanor herself had passed away unexpectedly in December 1933 and his second wife Constance Dudley, whom he had married in 1937, died a year later in 1940. The political legacy of the Aclands was now passed to the younger generation with Richard playing a prominent role in parliamentary affairs. The conversion of Richard to the cause of Christian Socialism meant that he left the Liberals in 1942 to form Common Wealth. This radical movement ignored the wartime truce between the main parties and gained three seats from the Conservatives in parliamentary by-elections. Labour's historic landslide in 1945 undermined the position of Common Wealth and Richard himself decided to join the Labour party. In 1947 he was returned to the House of Commons in a by-election at Gravesend but resigned from the party in 1955 over his opposition to the party leadership's support for the manufacture of the hydrogen bomb. He came third in the subsequent election as an Independent.[63] Geoffrey Acland, his younger brother, remained with the old Liberal cause. He contested the rural constituency of Westmorland for five successive elections from 1945 to 1959 and was able to consolidate the Liberal vote during the party's darkest days. Geoffrey's early death in 1964 brought an end to the family's active involvement in parliamentary politics. Yet this is also perhaps an appropriate point at which to complete this survey of the political traditions of the Acland family. By 1964 the Liberals were no longer in a state of long-term decline and this was particularly the case in Cornwall and Devon where the party was finally starting to recapture seats from the Conservatives. The cause that Francis and Eleanor had done so much to support throughout the early decades of the twentieth century had now made the psychological transition from despair to revival.

[61.] C. Cook and J. Ramsden (editors), *By-elections in British Politics,* London, 1993, p. 151; *Cornish Guardian,* 8 December 1938.
[62.] Tiverton Liberal Association papers, G/A1, executive committee minutes, 24 March and 15 April 1939.
[63.] Duncan Brack (editor), *Dictionary of Liberal Biography,* London, 1998, p. 3.

Liberalism and the Rise of Socialism

From a thematic angle many of the letters in the Acland collection relate to the breakthrough of the Labour party. At the local level the correspondence between Francis and Eleanor in the closing stages of the First World War highlights the surprising challenge of Labour in a region that might be regarded as a typical rural backwater for socialism. In reality Cornwall was to briefly emerge in 1918 as a potential Labour stronghold with its core in the old industrial heartland of the Mining Division. For Francis the answer to this challenge had to be co-operation with Labour rather than confrontation. This section outlines his local and national attempts to recast the old Progressive Alliance of the Edwardian period into a partnership that recognised the changing nature of British politics. In the immediate post-war period he attempted to play a pivotal role at Westminster in laying the foundations of a new 'Democratic party' that could rejuvenate the cause of progressive politics. The ultimate failure of this strategy, along with the implications for the strategic positioning of Liberalism, is then explored in the context of the changing nature of Liberal-Labour relations throughout the 1920s.

Looking first at the local level it should be noted that studies of Cornwall's political culture tend to focus on the failure of the Labour party to replace the Liberals as the main alternative to the Conservatives in the first half of the twentieth century.[64] Labour had certainly failed to undermine the supremacy of Cornish Liberalism during the crucial 'Age of Alignment' and it was not until 1945 that the party could even win a single seat in Cornwall. The survival of a strong Liberal tradition was to underpin an early revival in the mid-1950s that was eventually to lead to the parliamentary victories of popular candidates from Peter Bessell to David Penhaligon over the subsequent twenty years. One might add that the unique political evolution of the Duchy after the First World War is also significant in understanding the noteworthy success of the Liberal Democrats in completely monopolising Cornwall's parliamentary representation in the 2005 general election. In that sense the long-term failure of Labour to make a breakthrough in the inter-war period had serious implications. Although Labour had actually emerged as the second party in West Cornwall by the middle of the twentieth century and it was the Conservatives who were in any case the main party in the Duchy from 1931 to 1997, the critical

---

[64.] This includes G. Tregidga, 'The Survival of Cornish Liberalism, 1918–45'; *Journal of the Royal Institution of Cornwall*, 1992, pp. 211–32; A. Lee, 'Political Parties and Elections' in P. Payton (ed.), *Cornwall Since the War: The Contemporary History of a European Region*, Redruth, 1993, pp. 253–71; and P. Payton, 'Labour Failure and Liberal Tenacity: Radical Politics and Cornish Political Culture, 1880–1939' in P. Payton (ed.), *Cornish Studies: Two*, Exeter, 1994, pp. 83–96.

factor was that there was sufficient reality behind the myth of Liberal Cornwall to ensure that the Duchy could still be regarded as a relative stronghold of Liberalism. Yet the failure of Labour might be regarded as inevitable given the fact that socio-economic conditions did not appear suitable for socialism. Even senior figures in the local Labour movement had to concede by the late 1920s that it was in 'areas like Cornwall, where the population is so scattered, where individuality is . . . so ingrained, and where our creed and our programme are . . . imperfectly understood and appreciated, that we have our hardest task'.[65]

However, in the immediate aftermath of the First World War Cornwall was actually at the forefront in the rise of socialism. A remarkable feature of the 1918 general election was the respectable showing of Labour throughout West Cornwall with the party's candidates, Albert Dunn at St Ives and George Nicholls at Camborne, achieving good results with 38.4 and 48.0 per cent of the vote respectively. It was a sign of the times that both Dunn and Nicholls had been returned as Liberal MPs in the great Liberal landslide of 1906. Francis informed Asquith after the election that 'my return was rather a fluke for though I beat a good Labour man in a straight fight, I should not have won if the Tory candidate, who had not got back from India in time, had been put forward. . . . With a Tory standing Labour would win'.[66] What is even more surprising is the fact that Labour enjoyed greater success in Cornwall in 1918 than in some other parts of Britain more usually considered as socialist strongholds. By comparison both Sheffield and Stepney were to emerge as key Labour areas by the late 1920s, but in the first post-war election relatively low shares of the vote, roughly only a fifth to a third, were normal. Similarly, Labour's share of the vote in 1918 was actually greater in Camborne and St Ives than it was in future strongholds like Bermondsey, Doncaster, Aberavon and Motherwell. The result in Camborne, which now became a target seat for Labour, was even fractionally better than in Keir Hardie's old socialist citadel of Merthyr. Indeed, it seemed that West Cornwall was more likely to go Labour at the next election than other parts of Britain. Outside of the seats actually won in 1918 the Labour vote in Camborne was the sixth highest in the United Kingdom and St Ives came a respectable forty eighth out of a total of 325 seats.[67]

The early success of the Labour party in the Duchy was based on the local expansion of the trade union movement. For example, in 1914 the Workers' Union had just 400 members in Cornwall, but by 1918 membership had apparently risen to over 15,000 and the union was starting to

[65]. *Cornish Guardian,* 6 June 1929.
[66]. Asquith papers, MS. Asquith, fol. 34, Francis Acland to Herbert Asquith, 29 December 1918.
[67]. Calculations based on Craig, *British Parliamentary Election Results, 1918–1949.*

build on its core support in industrial areas by targeting agricultural labourers, particularly in the rural areas around Truro.[68] Camborne emerged as the powerhouse of the Labour movement in Cornwall. During the First World War the Workers' Union had been able to establish a 'strong and effective membership' in the constituency as wartime conditions enabled union activists to build up support amongst the two key groups of tin miners and munitions workers.[69] Apart from general factors for the wartime expansion of the Labour movement, there was also local resentment over the defeat of the clay strikers in 1913. Letters in the Acland collection highlight the tensions caused by the decision to bring down police units from Bristol and South Wales in order to control the strike. These external detachments were regarded locally as an 'army of occupation' and in September 1913 one of Francis's correspondents claimed that the strikers were starting to feel 'outcasts, with all society fighting against them'.[70] Resentment continued after the outbreak of the war with reports of a general reluctance to enlist in the army due to anti-establishment sentiment as a result of the strike. Indeed, army recruitment meetings in the Clay Country in 1914 were disrupted by the clay workers with shouts of 'What about twelve months ago? We don't forget'.[71] The political implications certainly appeared significant. S.C. Behenna, Cornwall organiser for the Workers' Union, remarked in 1918 that 'when he commenced his work in the county he was snubbed by the leaders of the two political parties; today those leaders were saying to him, "Behenna, shall we come on the platform with you?"' But the Labour movement was determined that its interests would not be represented after the war by the old parties. In February 1918 twenty trade unions and local co-operative associations held a meeting in Truro which called on Labour to contest every seat in Cornwall since 'they had no concern for either Liberal or Tory'.[72] The seriousness of the socialist challenge had been recognised in the previous year by Francis who claimed that the power of the Cornish Labour movement was at least equal to counties in the North of England more usually regarded as Labour strongholds:

> I'm in the dumps about it now because we only got 30 at the meeting in Redruth yesterday out of 200 [invitations] sent out. I think the Labour party have sent word round to the working men that they're not to come, and they feel proud of staying

[68] *Cornish Guardian*, 21 February 1918.
[69] *Western Morning News*, 2, 5, 12 and 16 December 1918.
[70] National Archives, HO 45/10710/242402, J.F. Williams to Francis Acland, 2 September 1913.
[71] S. Dalley, 'The Response in Cornwall to the Outbreak of the First World War' in P. Payton (ed.), *Cornish Studies: Eleven,* Exeter, 2003, p. 101.
[72] *Cornish Guardian*, 21 February 1918.

away. At nine meetings I've had under 300 people & I doubt if one could pick out nine villages in Yorks or Lancs where I should have had such a poor attendance.[73]

By the time of the 1918 general election it seemed unlikely that Acland would hold the seat. Even C.V. Thomas, a major employer in the mining industry and formerly a pivotal supporter of the Liberal cause, publicly refused to support him. Significantly, Thomas invited Arthur Henderson, the Labour party secretary and former chairman of the parliamentary party, to stay at his home during the election and at a constituency rally addressed by the socialist leader he expressed his 'full sympathy with the aims of Labour'.[74] The prospect of a Labour challenge also boosted the chances of the Conservative candidate, Captain G.F. Thomas-Peter. On the eve of the start of the election campaign Eleanor called on her husband to withdraw from the contest. She concluded that he had only a 'sporting chance' of victory and added that 'I can't help foreseeing how utterly miserable we should feel if Peter got in'.[75] By withdrawing in favour of Nicholls it would unite the progressive vote behind Labour and prevent a victory by the Conservatives who had already started campaigning in Camborne. In the event Peter's supporters were unable to contact him before nomination day since he was still travelling back from India, where he had been stationed in the army since 1914, and interestingly it was his wife who took the final decision that the Conservatives should withdraw from the contest.[76] Acland still felt that it was his duty to defend the seat. In a letter apparently written towards the end of the election campaign he declared that 'I've just about had as much as I could have stood of this but I'm glad we did it. It will at any rate keep our consciences good when we're outed – as I think we shall be'.[77]

It was understandable that Francis did not really enjoy the contest in Camborne. Suffering from bronchitis by the end of the campaign and unable to attend the declaration of the results, he also faced a serious opponent in Nicholls. Prior to the election Francis had indicated that in certain circumstances he might be prepared to stand aside in favour of the Labour party and this statement was exploited by Nicholls who claimed that Camborne was now natural Labour territory. He added that Acland was merely 'an academic politician' from the aristocratic elite who could not understand the daily struggle of the working class. Comparing their different backgrounds Nicholls argued that when 'my rival was grinding at his books I

---

73. Acland papers, 1148 M/667, Francis Acland to Eleanor Acland, late 1917.
74. *Cornish Post*, 14 December 1918.
75. Acland papers, 1148 M/124, Eleanor Acland to Francis Acland, late 1918.
76. *Cornish Post*, 30 November and 7 December 1918.
77. Acland papers, 1148 M/733, Francis Acland to Eleanor Acland, late 1918.

was struggling as a farm lad nine years of age. When my rival was keen on small holdings and the knowledge derived about them from books I was at work on one'.[78] His proactive style of campaigning also included the use of posters proclaiming that 'Labour won the War' in a bid to attract the patriotic vote. Forced on to the defensive Francis responded by focusing on the local needs of the mining industry in order to retain working-class support. He pointed out that his offer to stand aside in favour of Labour had been on the understanding that the party adopted a local candidate with 'practical experience' of the mining industry. Acland also claimed that his record in supporting the trade unions, along with his advocacy of state control of the local tin industry, meant that he was still the obvious champion of the Mining Division.[79] He was supported by Eleanor who proved to be an extremely capable politician in her own right. She targeted the new female voters, who were recognised as a pivotal group in the election, and dealt aggressively with hecklers from the Labour party. Despite Eleanor's concerns in a letter to Francis that she would not be able to speak freely about the main issues of the day, she was highly critical of the policies and approach of the Lloyd George Coalition. In particular she claimed that the coupon or pledge issued jointly by Lloyd George and Andrew Bonar Law, the leader of the Conservative party, to a restricted number of supporters undermined the independence of individual MPs and was further evidence of a growing threat to democracy itself:

> It is a monstrous shame that in this great country which has just freed Germany from the Hohenzollern yoke, that we should be asked to bind representatives to blindfold pledges. We stand, within the next two years to have a less free country than Germany herself, if we do not take care. Mr Acland will not pledge himself in that way: if you want a penny-in-the-slot member, you must vote for somebody else.[80]

Eleanor also revealed during the election campaign that both she and her husband had been offered other seats to contest. An underlying theme of her husband's letters in 1917 and 1918 was his growing wish to withdraw from Camborne. Although Francis's preference was to leave Cornwall and fight his home constituency of Tiverton, serious consideration was being given to the idea that he should replace Isaac Foot as the prospective Liberal candidate for Bodmin. In February 1918 C.A. Millman, the Liberal agent for Bodmin, wrote that Foot intended to withdraw in order to contest another seat, possibly in Plymouth, where the party had less chance of victory. With a young family and growing business commitments he was

---

[78.] *Cornish Post,* 23 November 1918.
[79.] *Ibid,* 30 November 1918.
[80.] *Ibid,* 30 November 1918.

unable to commit himself to a potentially winnable seat. Acland's progressive reputation, according to Millman, meant that he was the ideal choice to contest Bodmin in the Liberal interest.[81] Although no reply has been found from Acland, subsequent letters from Millman suggest that he had not ruled out the possibility. On 20 August, just three months before the election campaign, he was still hoping that it would be possible for Acland to contest Bodmin. He added that if 'you come I am absolutely confident we shall capture the seat'. Boundary changes appeared to indicate that the south-east Cornwall division, which had been a two-way marginal in the 1910 elections, was now more likely to be a 'safe seat for the Liberal party, providing that there [was] no intervention on the part of Labour'.[82] In the event Foot agreed to withdraw his resignation but it is worth speculating on the long-term implications for the Liberals if he had not stood in Bodmin. After all, the Foot tradition was to become central to the cultural memory of Cornish Liberalism following his famous by-election victory at Bodmin in 1922. Apart from laying the electoral foundations for the Liberal landslide in Cornwall in the following year, the symbolic nature of Foot's appeal to local interests like nonconformity was crucial in enabling the party to survive the challenge posed by the 'Age of Alignment'. The Millman letters indicate that this particular course of events, along with its long-term implications for the survival of Cornish Liberalism, was certainly not inevitable in the closing months of the First World War.

Just as likely at the time perhaps was Acland's own vision of a new progressive force in British politics. In July 1917 he declared that the 'one thing that seems to me certain is that at the next election and after we shall not know the old parties – Conservative, or Liberals, or Labour – any more as they have hitherto been known'.[83] An opportunity now existed for 'an entirely new division of parties' that could bring about a revival in progressive politics based on an equal partnership between Labour and the independent Liberals. Rather than the demise of organised Liberalism he envisaged a natural extension of the pre-war Lib-Lab pact, which had been responsible for the early expansion of the Labour party as a parliamentary force in the House of Commons. One of Eleanor's key arguments for her husband's withdrawal from Camborne in 1918 in support of Nicholls was that it would strengthen the possibility of 'a Lib.Lab coalition not merely for the constituency but for the whole country'. She added that this gesture would enhance Francis's reputation with the Labour movement enabling

---

[81.] Bodmin Liberal Association papers, Liskeard Liberal Democrat Office, copies of letters written during the First World War, C.A. Millman to Francis Acland, 21 February 1918.

[82.] *Ibid*, Millman to Francis Acland, 20 August 1918; Millman to Sir Francis Layland Barrett, 19 August 1918.

[83.] *Cornish Post*, 5 July 1917.

him to obtain the senior position of Foreign Secretary in the next Lib-Lab government.[84] Camborne was certainly seen as a pivotal seat at this time in local moves to construct a progressive alliance. One of the arguments used by Millman was that if Francis moved from Camborne to Bodmin it would pave the way for a Cornwall-wide agreement. This was essential since in August 1918 he warned that if the Mining division was lost to the Conservatives in a three-cornered contest it would serious undermine the wider Radical cause in Cornwall:

> It would be an excellent thing if we could come to some understanding . . . with the Labour party as to the Cornish seats. It is useless to close our eyes to existing conditions and to ignore their possible and probable developments. If we could with good grace give them one or two seats by intimating that we did not intend to contest them, we should make our position absolutely safe and sure with regard to the remaining three seats. . . . The offer of one seat might very easily satisfy the Labour party in this county, and Camborne is just the seat where they could, even in a triangular contest put up a stiff fight, and probably present the seat to the Tory party. Such a course would be a distinct blow to the progressive and democratic interests in this county.[85]

Paradoxically, the eventual victory of Francis at Camborne in 1918 was to provide him with a unique opportunity to advance the cause of a Lib-Lab alliance at Westminster. The defeat of Asquith, along with other prominent members of the party, meant that the independent Liberal group in the House of Commons now lacked any real leadership. The significance of this situation was not lost on Acland who pointed out to Asquith immediately after the declaration of results that he was the 'only survivor of those who remained faithful to you who served . . . in the first Coalition' with the Conservatives in 1915.[86] His offer to help co-ordinate the activities of the surviving members of the party until Asquith could win a seat was clearly a bid to establish himself as the obvious choice to lead the Liberals in the House of Commons. Acland's advocacy of a Lib-Lab alliance at least meant that he could offer the party a clear sense of direction. In a letter to Eleanor he claimed that reunion with the Lloyd George faction was no longer possible and since the Liberal party was in any case 'much too dead to make anything of itself as a real governing & directing force' the way forward was for the independent Liberals to work closely with Labour towards the ultimate objective of creating a new 'democratic party' in

---

[84.] Acland papers, 1148 M/124, Eleanor Acland to Francis Acland, late 1918.
[85.] Bodmin Liberal Association papers, Millman to E.C. Perry, 13 August 1918.
[86.] Asquith papers, fol. 34, Francis Acland to Herbert Asquith, 29 December 1918.

British politics.[87] By organising policy committees and study circles 'on the big issues of the future' the party could make an intellectual contribution to the formation of such a force. Running parallel to this new role as a ginger group Francis envisaged a practical partnership in the House of Commons with the Radical Liberals voting regularly with Labour against the Lloyd George Coalition.[88]

In the event, however, Asquith proposed Sir Donald Maclean as the temporary chairman of the parliamentary party. In his letter to Asquith in the aftermath of the 1918 election Francis had not even mentioned Maclean in his list of the most 'useful' members of the independent Liberal group. Maclean was certainly not the obvious choice since his only experience of serving in government was in 1911 as a lowly Parliamentary Private Secretary to the Master of Elibank, the Liberal Chief Whip.[89] Francis's grudging comment to Eleanor upon reading about the appointment in the newspapers was that the new chairman 'will be respectable – if not brilliant. It means that I lost my chance of doing it by being slack about all [House of Commons] things for the last two years'. Francis consoled himself with the view that 'Maclean's leadership will not dispose of my chief point which is that five or six of us should work steadily and constantly in close touch with Labour'.[90] Interestingly, Francis now played a key role in events at Westminster by chairing the meeting on 3 February 1919 that took the momentous decision to form a separate Independent or Free Liberal group in the House of Commons. This was no foregone conclusion since some individuals like George Lambert, the MP for South Molton, favoured closer links with Lloyd George, while Francis's natural allies on the left, including Wedgwood Benn and Sydney Arnold, preferred a new grouping rather than the continuation of the 'old Lib party' under Asquith. Francis was able to steer the meeting towards an agreement and this resulted in Maclean being confirmed as the sessional chairman of the Free Liberals.[91] In retrospect it was a significant meeting since at this critical time in the party's history it could so easily have disappeared as an independent force. Moreover, on the surface it appears that both Asquith and Maclean were prepared to endorse the view advocated by Francis and others for an alliance with Labour. As Wilson points out, in the immediate post-war period both men

[87.] Acland papers, 1148 M/778, Francis Acland to Eleanor Acland, early 1919?
[88.] *Ibid*, 1148 M/782, Francis Acland to Eleanor Acland, early 1919?
[89.] R. Douglas in Brack (ed.), *Dictionary of Liberal Biography* concluded that up until the election debacle of 1918 'everything in his career suggested that he was living a useful public life which would one day merit an obituary notice in *The Times,* but would hardly bring him into the front rank of politics' (p. 242).
[90.] Acland papers, 1148 M/784, Francis Acland to Eleanor Acland, January 1919.
[91.] *Ibid*, 1148 M/785, Francis Acland to Eleanor Acland, 4 February 1919.

'believed that the next government would be composed of Liberals and Labour'.[92]

Yet the course of events that took place in early 1919 also goes someway to explaining the ultimate failure to establish a strong relationship with Labour. After all, Asquith chose Maclean because of his caution and conservatism rather than an ability to forge a radical movement on the centre-left of British politics. Stephen Koss points out that during his premiership he had 'made a speciality of reconciling the differences that arose among his subordinates'.[93] His instinctive response following the defeat of 1918 was to seek a compromise solution that would enable him to remain in control of the party. This can be seen in relation to a letter written by Francis after the election in which he recounts that Asquith had invited Lambert and himself to a meeting to see if 'we objected to D.Maclean' as chairman.[94] As the two senior Privy Councillors in the parliamentary group both men had a greater claim to the post than Maclean but significantly they were associated with the rival wings of the party. Notwithstanding Francis's own view that the reason he failed to obtain the chairmanship was his performance in the House of Commons, the underlying factor behind the choice of Maclean was that he was more closely aligned with the moderate approach favoured by Asquith. Lambert was apparently unhappy that he had been overlooked as chairman and subsequently moved over to the Lloyd George camp. However, the conciliatory line of Asquith on the subject of closer links with Labour was sufficient to win the support of Francis who wrote to Eleanor that he had 'established most friendly relations with Maclean, Gulland [the former Liberal Chief Whip] & Asquith'. He convinced himself that he was now part of the inner circle of the party with 'a position of usefulness – and without too much responsibility'.[95] In reality the actions of the Asquith-Maclean leadership were hardly likely to win over the Labour party. The *Times* concluded that the inaugural meeting chaired by Francis had been held with the specific purpose of challenging the claim of the Labour party that it was now 'the official Opposition'.[96] From the start Asquith was determined the maintain the independent identity of the party and Maclean's move to occupy seats on the Front Bench at the opening of parliament was intended as a symbolic challenge to Labour. Such tactics had the effect of further blurring the strategic and ideological position of the Free Liberals in the years after the First World War. As Chris Cook put it, '[t]he first – and basic – task for the Liberal Party was to decide where it stood in relation to Labour. This, in

[92.] Wilson, *Downfall of the Liberal Party,* p. 217.
[93.] Koss, *Asquith,* p. 99 and 177.
[94.] Acland papers, 1148 M/780, Francis Acland to Eleanor Acland, January 1919?
[95.] *Ibid.*
[96.] *Times,* 8 and 24 January 1919.

the six years after 1918, Asquith and his supporters never established'.[97]

Only a proactive approach towards political realignment had any chance of success. Significantly, the radical wing of the Free Liberals recognised that Asquith's cautious but autocratic leadership was an obstacle to change. At the inaugural meeting in February 1919 James Hogge had challenged Asquith's appointment of George Thorne, another close ally, as the group's new Chief Whip. It was claimed that 'no man . . . could be a leader of the party and remain outside the House of Commons'.[98] Such a strident demand for greater internal democracy could not be ignored and it resulted in a compromise with Hogge and Thorne acting as joint whips. One might add that this event was Francis's lost opportunity. As the senior Radical amongst the surviving Free Liberals he was well placed to lead a wider rebellion with the aim of wresting the leadership away from Asquith. His personal links with members of the Labour party, combined with a reputation as a radical politician, meant that he was the obvious choice to lead a streamlined Radical group in association with Labour. Furthermore, the period immediately after the 1918 election provided a unique opportunity to demonstrate the benefits of such a strategy. During the spring of 1919 the Liberals won three by-election victories at the expense of the Conservatives. Only a disappointing performance in a three-cornered contest at Rusholme in October pointed to the underlying weakness of Liberalism and heralded a major by-election challenge by the Labour party in its own right.[99] Yet insights from the letters also highlight the reasons why Francis was unable to exploit this situation to his own advantage. Although well aware of the inadequacies of Asquith as leader, his emphasis on duty and loyalty meant that he was hardly likely to lead a grassroots rebellion. Moreover, he was clearly frustrated at this time by what he felt were his own failings as a politician and this lack of confidence meant that he was unable to seize the initiative and move the party in a new direction at a critical stage in its history.[100]

By 1924 the nature of the relationship between the Liberal and Labour parties had changed once again. On a superficial level there was now an opportunity for both parties to work together since Labour was in office for the first time but dependent on Liberal support. Francis, now the Member for Tiverton, was still enthusiastic about the chances for a progressive partnership. Even in the difficult circumstances of the October 1924 election he took the brave decision to emphasise the positive benefits of the two parties working together and emphasised in his election address that he

[97.] Cook, *Age of Alignment,* p. 226.
[98.] *Times,* 4 February 1919.
[99.] Cook, *Age of Alignment,* pp. 9–10.
[100.] Acland papers, 1148 M/784, Francis Acland to Eleanor Acland, January 1919; 1148 M/781, Francis Acland to Eleanor Acland, early 1919.

had supported the government's budget along with their foreign policy, an 'extension of Old Age Pensions, . . . the Housing Act, and the setting up of Agricultural Wages Committees'.[101] Nonetheless, even Francis seemed to be moving away from the earlier goal of a new 'Democratic party'. In his address to the electors of Tiverton he presented Liberalism as the safe, middle option in contrast to the extremes of Conservatism and Socialism. Such sentiments might have been in line with mainstream Liberal opinion but it really symbolised the triumph of Asquithian vagueness rather than a bright new future on the centre-left of British politics. However, by 1926 internal divisions were leading progressives like Eleanor to consider the possibility of a new party led by Lloyd George and 'reasonable' members of the Labour party. In the aftermath of the General Strike it was a tempting option to seek realignment by launching a breakaway movement funded by the former Prime Minister's political fund. It appears that in June 1926 Francis actually joined Lloyd George and other leading progressives for a weekend gathering at Churt 'to discuss a programme for a new party'.[102]

Popular support for Lloyd George in his power struggle with Asquith temporarily removed the need for a breakaway progressive force. But on the other hand it should be noted that the long-term implications of the Liberal party's frustrated search for a realignment in centre-left politics also contributed to its demise. With even moderates like Asquith and Maclean claiming that their natural ally was Labour the party seemed psychologically unprepared to fight on two fronts. This was a point raised by Eleanor following the disappointing results of the 1929 election. In her view the party was still campaigning in the same way that it had done before the war when Conservatism was the principal enemy. She added that a new threat to freedom and liberty had emerged in the form of Labour but this had not been recognised in the party's desire to focus on the failings of the Baldwin government. By ignoring the implications of three-party politics they had paradoxically made 'converts not only to Liberalism but to the fiercer form of anti-Toryism, namely, "Labour"'.[103] From that perspective the implications were significant. Not only were the Liberals unable to forge a close post-war alliance with Labour; the legacy of progressive politics meant that throughout the 1920s the party was emotionally unable to counter the socialist challenge. This was even more of a problem by 1929 because of the increase in the number of three-cornered contests. In the early 1920s many Liberals, especially in rural areas, had enjoyed straight fights with the Conservatives, but the so-called

---

[101.] National Liberal Club collection, University of Bristol Library, DM 668, 1924 election address of Francis Acland for the Tiverton constituency.
[102.] Acland papers, 1148 M/1086, Eleanor Acland to Richard Acland, 23 May 1926; 1148 M/1088, Eleanor Acland to Richard Acland, 3 June 1926.
[103.] *Liberal Women's News,* June 1929, p. 42.

'Socialist incursion' at the end of the decade marked the end of the pre-war Conservative-Liberal alignment that still existed in some seats. This was particularly the case in the South West of Britain where the Liberals had won the largest number of seats in 1923 as a result of straight fights with the Conservatives. In 1929 the party could make only isolated gains at South Molton and East Dorset due to the increase in the number of Labour candidates.[104] A good example was Richard Acland's failure to win Torquay. In 1923 the Liberals had narrowly gained the seat by 372 votes in a straight fight with the Conservatives. By the end of the decade, however, the mere presence of a Labour candidate was undermining the Liberal position. Quite apart from allowing the sitting Conservative MP to retain the seat on a minority vote, Eleanor claimed that the local socialist challenger, though never having 'a chance of winning, . . . frightened some of the more timid voters' into supporting the Conservatives.[105] Only in Cornwall, which had seemed on the verge of becoming a Labour stronghold in 1918, did the Liberals survive this challenge on two fronts by winning all five seats. Even Camborne, which Francis had assumed was likely to go socialist in the near future, was still represented by a Liberal in 1929. In order to understand this somewhat surprising turnaround in the fortunes of Liberalism the final part of this introduction will move away from a macro focus to a consideration of the provincial nature of British politics after 1910 with a particular focus on Cornwall.

Politics in the Provinces

With independent Liberalism struggling to survive after the First World War in a political system increasingly polarised between Labour and the Conservatives it is understandable that historians have tended to focus on events occurring in state politics rather than in the provinces. Yet the pioneering work of Scandinavian political scientist, Stein Rokkan, in relation to centre-periphery politics demonstrated the complexities of political change at the local level. Rokkan's personal research was based on the experience of Scandinavia where socialist parties, the New Left, had established an early supremacy at the state level because of support in urban and industrial areas. In some remote parts of the Nordic countryside, however, the predominance of small farms, the relative strength of religious nonconformity and an essentially 'egalitarian class structure' preserved a traditional political culture more conducive for Old Left parties like the Liberals. The political dynamics of a strong sub-state culture tended to be associated with three

104. For a discussion of this subject see Tregidga, *Liberal Party in South-West Britain*, pp. 50–55.
105. *Western Morning News,* 14 May 1929.

core factors: a belief that the economic needs of rural communities were ignored by urban-based parties; the anti-metropolitan hostility of a subject province; and the political agenda of religious nonconformity.[106] Voters at the sub-state level could therefore be subject to conflicting influences with the dominant cleavage, class politics or local issues, shifting from election to election. The political correspondence of the Aclands indicates that these factors should be considered in relation to British politics. At one level this can be seen in regard to the perception in rural areas that Westminster was neglecting the interests of agriculture in favour of urban Britain. Territorial politics must also be considered with anti-metropolitan debates in Cornwall reflecting wider developments taking place in the larger Celtic nations of Scotland and Wales. Given the changing political environment of the inter-war period these provincial cleavages appeared to offer an alternative role for the Liberals at a time of realignment. This final section will also consider Francis's own political personality in relation to issues of provincial politics.

Agricultural reform was an important subject for Francis. His experience as a wartime government minister at the Board of Agriculture and Fisheries, combined with the family's existing reputation as progressive landowners, meant that this interest was only to be expected. In February 1917 he was briefing Asquith on the Coalition's likely policies in this area but his subsequent annoyance at the former Prime Minister's failure to respond suggests that the land was not really a priority for all Liberals at this stage.[107] By 1923, however, the Liberals could not afford to ignore agriculture since the party's decline in urban and industrial Britain meant that it was dependent on the rural constituencies in order to survive. This support was significant since in the election of that year the Liberals actually captured half of the parliamentary seats where the agricultural interest represented more than 30 per cent of the working male population.[108] Indeed, it is possible to see these victories as reflecting the hidden importance of the rural-urban issue in British politics. Although the Conservatives have tended to be regarded as the defenders of the agricultural interest, the potential for realignment went further than just a simple process of Labour replacing the Liberals as the principal centre-left party. With the Conservatives actually losing ground in rural areas there was always the possibility that the Liberals could have taken on that mantle and copied the model of the centrist Agrarian parties of Scandinavia. Francis recognised the possibilities of

---

[106.] S. Rokkan, *Citizens: Elections: Parties: Approaches to the Comparative Study of the Processes of Development,* Oslo, 1970, pp. 72–144.

[107.] Asquith papers, Bodleian Library, Francis Acland to Herbert Asquith, 18 February 1917; Acland papers, 1148/M/ 655, Francis Acland to Eleanor Acland, February 1917.

[108.] M. Kinnear, *The British Voter: An Atlas and Survey since 1885,* London, 1968, p. 120.

developing a programme based on agricultural issues. In 1924 his electoral address in Tiverton emphasised that a policy based on 'the best use of the land' offered an attractive platform that could appeal to supporters of all three parties.[109] However, the problem for the Liberals was that the Conservatives had been able to pose as the real champions of the rural interest when they were in opposition in 1924. Anti-socialist sentiment in rural areas meant that the Liberal party, which was perceived as the parliamentary ally of the MacDonald administration, was vulnerable to a Conservative revival in the 1924 election. In a speech in the neighbouring seat of Taunton the Conservative leader, Stanley Baldwin, was able to seize the initiative on land by warning that another Labour administration would lead to further bureaucratic interference from Whitehall. Above all, he positioned his party as the natural champions of the agricultural interest in the urban-rural divide:

> There has grown up in the towns during the last generation or more large vested interests in the handling and distribution of foreign foodstuffs who will fight to the death against any im-provement of rural conditions that will lessen their prospects of trade. We have also to reckon with the ignorance that exists in urban districts about country life, and that in itself is a serious thing. This country is almost split up into two nations – the urban and the rural.[110]

Nonetheless, Francis still believed that the land held the key to a Liberal revival. His association with Lloyd George in the latter part of the decade gave him an opportunity to influence the development of party policy on this subject. Lloyd George believed that with Labour still a weak force in many county constituencies the Liberals had a unique opportunity to strengthen their 'grasp on the rural districts' at the next election in order to win a minimum of 100 seats in the House of Commons. With a secure bloc of seats the party would then be in a position to present itself as the alternative to Labour 'if Toryism breaks down'.[111] The Liberals came fairly close to success in the first stage of this strategy. In 1929 the party won 59 seats but there were 19 county constituencies in Britain where the lead of the winning candidate over the Liberal was less than 4.0 per cent and 27 vulnerable to an additional swing of up to 3.0 per cent.[112] As Eleanor recognised, the intervention of a greater number of Labour candidates was crucial in limiting the Liberal advance. But the party itself was also respons-

[109] National Liberal Club collection, DM 668, 1924 election address of Francis Acland.

[110] *Times,* 18 October 1924.

[111] A.M. Dawson, 'Politics in Devon and Cornwall, 1900–31', PhD thesis, University of London, 1991.

[112] Calculations based on Craig, *British Parliamentary Election Results, 1918–1949.*

ible since the divisions that followed the launch of Lloyd George's land campaign at Killerton meant that the rural programme was effectively sidelined by the time of the election. By not pursuing their original intention of focusing on the countryside the party lacked a means of targeting rural Britain. Lloyd George's famous pledge to conquer unemployment was in many ways irrelevant in terms of electoral strategy since it was targeted at the industrial and urban areas, which had already moved over in many cases to Labour. Vital votes might well have been lost in the key agricultural marginals through the flawed nature of Liberal strategy. Even in the 1930s, however, Francis had not abandoned the view that a rural programme was the answer to the party's problems. At the Blickling Hall conference in October 1932 the Liberals discussed a range of options in order to reverse their continuing decline. As De Groot pointed out, for Francis the answer was still 'a rural radicalism which would wrest control of the countryside from the Conservatives'.[113] Given the evidence for regional diversity in inter-war British politics there is a need for such views to be considered within new research on rural Liberalism.

Rokkan's work suggests that rural discontent also needs to be studied alongside wider issues of territorial politics. In a British context a useful starting point is the Liberal split of 1886 over home rule for Ireland which had led Gladstone and his supporters to make the 'Irish Question' more relevant to mainland Britain. This was particular the case in Scotland and Wales where anti-metropolitan sentiment was clearly evident amongst Liberal MPs and constituency associations before 1914 in regard to political devolution ('Home Rule All Round'), long-term socio-economic problems in peripheral areas and religious issues like the disestablishment of the Anglican church in Wales. The process continued after the First World War. Running parallel to the inter-war 'Age of Alignment' in Celtic Britain was the creation of Plaid Cymru in 1925 and the National Party of Scotland, a predecessor of the Scottish National Party, in 1928.[114] Both parties enjoyed little electoral success during the inter-war period but significantly a nationalist tradition had now been established as an alternative to West-minster politics during a critical period of electoral change. Anti-metropoli-tanism was also present in Cornish politics. Before considering the views of Francis it is instructive to consider the local background which suggests that in the years leading up to the First World War there had been a gradual fusion of Celtic imagery and anti-metropolitan issues within the framework

[113.] G. J. De Groot, *Liberal Crusader: The Life of Sir Archibald Sinclair,* London, 1993, p. 98.

[114.] H.J. Hanham, *Scottish Nationalism,* London, 1969, pp. 99–107; T.G. Jones, 'E.T. John and Welsh Home Rule, 1910–14', *The Welsh History Review,* Vol. 13, 1987, pp. 453–67; L. McAllister, *Plaid Cymru: The Emergence of a Political Party,* Bridgend, 2001.

of the dominant Liberal-Nonconformist nexus in Cornwall. Even in the mid-nineteenth century the propagandists campaigning for a Cornish diocese had claimed that the Duchy was entitled to a separate status on the grounds of its Celtic heritage.[115] Cornwall was still sometimes described as West Wales and when Lloyd George visited Falmouth on an election visit in January 1910 he declared that the Cornish and the Welsh shared the 'same Celtic passion for liberty'. He described the meeting, to the cheers of the crowd, as a 'gathering of his fellow [Celtic] countrymen'.[116] Such sentiments were exploited by leading Liberals like Sir Arthur Quiller-Couch, chairman of the Bodmin constituency association, in order to provide a pan-Celtic defence of the unpopular policy of Irish Home Rule.[117]

Indeed, there is evidence at this time to suggest that the Liberals were starting to construct a Cornish agenda that could imitate the growing political demands of Wales, Scotland and Ireland. The Welsh Disestablish-ment Bill of 1912 led Carkeek to call for a similar measure to disestablish the Anglican Church in Cornwall on the grounds that the Methodists were the dominant religious force in the Duchy. In the same year Cornish MPs like Acland and T.C. Robartes claimed that local issues ranging from leasehold enfranchisement to the economic problems of the fishing industry were being ignored by central government.[118] At his adoption meeting in November 1910 Francis had even raised the possibility of Cornish Home Rule, albeit in a somewhat light-hearted manner, alongside devolution for the larger nations of England, Scotland and Wales.[119] This federal prog-ramme of creating a comprehensive structure of local Parliaments through-out Britain would follow the immediate goal of Home Rule for Ireland. When Winston Churchill called in 1912 for devolution to be extended to the regions of England on the basis of the old Anglo Saxon Heptarchy the constitutional implications for Cornwall with its historical claims as a Celtic nation, combined with the economic legacy of the collapse of the mining industry in the late nineteenth century, were seriously discussed in local newspapers. Alfred Browning Lyne, the editor of the *Cornish Guardian* and an influential Liberal activist, declared that the 'Metropolis was coming to mean everything'. He saw no reason 'why Cornwall should not join in the "Regionalist" movement which is striving in various parts of Western Europe to revive local patriotism' and added that self-government for areas like Cornwall would provide a positive alternative to the 'excessive centralisation' of the British state:

115. P.S. Morrish, 'History, Celticism and propaganda in the formation of the diocese of Truro', *Southern History,* Vol. 5, 1983, pp. 238–66.
116. *West Briton,* 7 and 13 January 1910.
117. *Cornish Guardian,* 16 December 1910.
118. *Royal Cornwall Gazette,* 24 February 1910 and 29 February 1912.
119. *The Cornubian,* 1 December 1910.

Cornwall seems to be regarded 'up the country' as a rather insignificant place, more or less 'off the map'. There may be an idea that we have some sort of local problems – perhaps it is thought the natives eat a missionary now and then – but it would be far beneath the dignity of the Imperial Parliament to concern itself with these things. Here, surely, is a case where that delegation of power suggested by Mr. Churchill might be justified.[120]

Yet Cornish politics lacked a 'Parnell' or a 'Lloyd George' who could provide the inspirational leadership that was necessary to make the cultural transition from patriotism to nationalism. The parliamentary career of Robartes, who declared in 1910 that the 'chief characteristic of Cornishmen is their love of independence. As a nation we dislike being trampled on', came to a premature end in 1915 when he was killed in action on the Western Front.[121] Francis Acland was certainly no substitute leader for the embryonic cause of Cornish nationalism. On one level he comes across as a conscientious MP who recognised the importance of keeping in contact with his constituency. Indeed, at critical events, such as the outbreak of the First World War and the political crisis of December 1916, Francis provided regular reports on developments through a series of public letters to local newspapers. At Tiverton in the early 1920s he proved quite adept at presenting himself as the natural spokesman of the constituency. This can be seen in election addresses of the period, which emphasised that Francis 'and his family are and have been for generations among the best-known and best respected residents in the Division'.[122] As was pointed out earlier, his advocacy of rural radicalism in the inter-war period also showed he did not always think in terms of a state role for Liberalism. Yet there were limitations to Francis's ability to exploit local issues since his overriding concern was for high politics. In 1917 Herbert Thomas, the editor of the *Cornish Post*, gave an apt description of him as 'an able and conscious specimen of the cultured and trained hereditary Parliamentary official and administrator'.[123] He came from a family that saw politics more in relation to statewide domestic concerns like education and social reform rather than anti-metropolitan sentiment. One might add that this also posed wider problems for the Liberals as they made the uncomfortable transition to third party status. Notwithstanding the party's long-term commitment to issues like Home Rule for Ireland, its underlying concern after the First World War remained the goal of the 'next Liberal government' at Westminster.

120. *Cornish Guardian*, 6 and 20 September 1912.
121. *West Briton*, 7 and 21 January 1910.
122. National Liberal Club collection, DM 668, 1924 election address of Francis Acland.
123. *Cornish Post*, 5 July 1917.

A good example of Francis's relative indifference to provincial politics was his reluctance to oppose the reduction in Cornwall's parliamentary representation from seven to five members as a result of the 1918 Reform Act. A year earlier there had been widespread opposition amongst all parties towards the regional recommendations of the boundary commission. Apart from an overall reduction in the number of Cornish seats in the House of Commons, there was concern that the new boundaries did not allow for the historic link between parliamentary representation and local industries.[124] There was a traditional assumption at the local level that the St Austell seat in Mid Cornwall reflected the interests of the China Clay industry. Similarly, fishing was associated with St Ives in the west, agriculture with Bodmin and North Cornwall in the east and mining with Camborne. Yet the 1917 proposals threatened this relationship. This was particularly the case in regard to the Mining Division, which was to be renamed and attached to the small borough of Penryn & Falmouth. Local councils, along with prominent Conservatives like J.C. Williams and Labour activists under the leadership of Sam Jacobs, a hero of the 1913 Clay Strike, decided to organise a petition in favour of a compromise measure of six seats.[125] This proposal would ensure the survival of the Mining Division and allow for the separate representation of the other key economic interests of the Duchy. Ironically the Cornish Liberals had apparently been the original 'pioneers of the six-seat scheme'. However, Francis played a pivotal role in undermining the chances of an all-party alliance by declaring in a public letter to the local press that 'Liberals were honourably bound not to try to disturb the redistribution proposals'. With Cornwall's other Liberal MPs generally loyal to the Lloyd George Coalition the anti-redistribution campaign needed Acland's support to mount an effective challenge. Significantly, other leading Liberals like Carkeek and Lyne now echoed Acland's view that given the government's commitment to increasing the number of seats in other areas of Britain it was inevitable that Cornwall's representation would be reduced to just five seats.[126]

Yet the anti-redistribution campaign in Cornwall was significant for the way in which it articulated regionalist discontent. Reginald F. Reynolds, who had been associated with the pre-war Celtic movement, claimed that the Cornish had been 'struggling to find expressions of their views' until the emergence of the threat to the Duchy's representation. He added that 'Home Rule reigns in the hearts of the Cornish' and saw the issue as a unique opportunity to 'put the Cornish case' to Westminster. The official petition document of the anti-redistribution campaign called on central

[124] *Ibid,* 14, 21, 28 June and 5 July 1917; *Royal Cornwall Gazette,* 21 February 1918.
[125] *Cornish Post,* 12 July 1917.
[126] *Ibid,* 5, 12 and 26 July 1917.

government 'to grant them a one and undivided Cornwall which will satisfy all local interests, aspirations and feelings'.[127] Moreover, the issue appeared to raise the need for a separate constitutional accommodation for the Duchy. In a letter to the local press Francis claimed that an exception could not be made for Cornwall since redistribution had to be applied fairly throughout the United Kingdom. He added that 'I see no other ways – do you? – for I am sure you do not really believe that this can be dealt with solely as a Cornish question'.[128] However, the central argument of the anti-distributionists was that Cornwall should copy the model advocated in relation to the 'Irish Question'. It was claimed that in 1885 Gladstone had defended the principle of greater representation for Ireland on the grounds that the more remote parts of the United Kingdom required special treatment since they were so far from London. This precedent now needed to be applied to Cornwall.[129] Ironically it was the Cornish Unionists, who were opposed to the wider concept of devolution, who now became associated with the anti-distributionist cause. Once again it was evident that Cornwall lacked a political leader with the imagination and understanding to exploit the full potential of the situation from a nationalist perspective.

Francis certainly recognised that he could benefit on a personal level from the Redistribution issue. In July 1917 he wrote that 'I am quite aware that I might become the most popular man in the Duchy by running a campaign that Cornwall is of such special importance that there must be no reduction of the present membership. But this is not a time for bothering about personal popularity'.[130] Such high-minded sentiments reflect his image as a honourable Member of Parliament who laid great stress on the need for the political process to be conducted on the principles of loyalty and responsibility, especially at a time of war. Much to his annoyance, however, the local Unionist press suggested that his failure to defend the interests of both Camborne and Cornwall was because he favoured the enlargement of the Mining Division in order to limit the threat from Labour. Although Francis strenuously denied the claim that he had a 'personal motive' for not opposing the redistribution proposals, his private letters to Eleanor indicate that there was an alternative reason for his stance. However, rather than seeing a larger division as a way of dividing the opposition, the real explanation was that he actually welcomed redistribution as an excuse for leaving Cornwall. By 1917 Francis was increasingly annoyed by local requests that he should increase the level of his annual financial donation to the Camborne Liberal Association. By the end of the war he was paying an annual subscription of £300 and this was particularly disappointing for

127. *Ibid*, 12 July 1917.
128. *Ibid*, 5 July 1917.
129. *Ibid*, 14 June 1917.
130. *Ibid*, 5 July 1917.

somebody who was an advocate of 'Democratic Finance', a system whereby all party members would help to generate the association's income in order to encourage more working-class candidates.[131] Writing in June 1917 Francis concluded that the incorporation of Penryn & Falmouth, which had tended to favour extremely wealthy Liberal candidates in the past, would 'be a good chance for me to make my own [financial] terms or move elsewhere . . . I think that very likely they will say "no" which would give me a decent excuse for getting out & going elsewhere'.[132]

Financial considerations were not the only reason for wanting to leave Camborne. From the beginning there is evidence to suggest that the electors of the Mining Division regarded Francis as a rather detached and aloof figure. A revealing insight into popular perceptions of his character and reputation can actually be seen in an essentially sympathetic account of his December 1910 campaign. Francis was described by *The Cornubian* as the 'outstanding figure in the Cornish contests' whose oratory was 'exact speech, mathematically accurate, closely reasoned, crystalline, with never a redundant word, nor an idea over expressed'. The paper added that 'not a few men with the reputation of being great Parliamentary orators have come into Cornwall to find that their eloquence is foreign to the locality, for Cornishmen have a Celtic love of fervid speech'. Francis, on the other hand, displayed a 'Parliamentary style to perfection' that could only be compared to the debating skills of Asquith.[133] In other words his precise style of speech meant that he was well respected as a statesman who seemed destined for high office but at the same time he lacked the passion and emotion that appealed to the Cornish whether in the chapel pulpit or on the political platform. During the war Francis frequently complained to his wife that the electorate saw them as 'high & mighty & unapproachable' and it reinforced his desire to retire from Camborne at the earliest opportunity.[134] Moreover, his annoyance with the Cornish for not accepting him as an equal started to take on racial overtones during the war years. This included patronising comments about 'their present state of development' and the lack of 'any sign that the people regard themselves as citizens'.[135]

His criticism was also directed at the moral agenda of Cornish Methodism. Given the significance of the Methodist vote in Camborne this meant that Francis could not afford to ignore core issues like temperance. For

[131.] Bodmin Liberal Association papers, Millman to Francis Acland, 21 February 1918; *Liberal Women's News,* January 1925, p. 25.
[132.] Acland papers, 1148 M/669, Francis Acland to Eleanor Acland, 3 June 1917.
[133.] *Cornubian,* 1 December 1910.
[134.] Acland papers. 1148 M/777, Francis Acland to Eleanor Acland, 9 October 1917; 1148 M/760, Francis Acland to Eleanor Acland, February 1918.
[135.] *Ibid,* 1148 M/776, Francis Acland to Eleanor Acland, 12 October 1917.

example, in July 1917 he expressed his support for the 'control and regulation of the drink traffic after the war'. Even when he moved to Hexham in 1929 his electoral address stressed that the 'Evils connected with the Drink Traffic can be overcome'.[136] Once again, however, such a policy was a distraction for Francis who wanted the electors of the Mining Division to focus on major issues of foreign policy and post-war reconstruction. Whilst his letters to Eleanor tend to be concerned with matters of high politics, he was forced to admit that the only issue that bothered his constituents was how to best tackle the 'Drink Question'. This might seem surprising given the tendency for historians to conclude that wartime conditions meant that religious issues 'suddenly seemed irrelevant both now and for the future'.[137] Yet in Cornwall it could be said that the war actually stimulated a renewed desire to champion the cause of traditional nonconformity. C. V. Thomas, speaking at Camborne in March 1918, claimed that 'a moral rot was getting into the British people and he . . . saw signs of this in the House of Commons', while Liberals in mid-Cornwall called on the government to tackle sexual immorality by suppressing 'the dens of infamy in the city of Cairo, where thousands of our British and Colonial soldiers have contracted venereal disease'.[138] Even the sanctity of the Sabbath was now threatened with many nonconformist farmers in Cornwall opposing government proposals to work their farms on Sundays.[139] In these circumstances there was a growing sentiment in the Duchy that 'sin' was both the cause and product of the war. This was particularly the case in regard to temperance with Millman claiming in an address to the Quethiock Rechabites in January 1918 that the liquor trade was a greater enemy to the country than Germany itself. A series of public meetings throughout the Duchy called for the radical solution of total prohibition for the duration of the war and for at least six months thereafter. Liberal activists in the Carthew polling district of the St Austell constituency even passed a resolution declaring that their continued support for Sir Francis Layland Barratt, the local Liberal MP, was 'conditional upon his advocacy of prohibition'.[140]

Francis admitted in a letter to the local press that his moderate line on temperance was not popular with Liberal activists. His vague comments about hoping that the government would 'carry through by general consent some measure' to control the liquor trade after the war was clearly never

[136.] *Cornish Post*, 21 June 1917; National Liberal Club collection, DM 668, 1929 election address of Francis Acland.

[137.] Wilson, *Downfall of the Liberal Party*, p. 24.

[138.] *West Briton*, 28 March 1918; *Royal Cornwall Gazette*, 17 January 1918.

[139.] *Cornish Post*, 22 March and 12 April 1917.

[140.] *Royal Cornwall Gazette*, 10 and 17 January 1918; *West Briton*, 30 October 1916, 21 December 1916 and 28 March 1918.

going to be enough for those temperance reformers who wanted immediate action.[141] Disenchanted with a people that, as Francis saw it, seemed to believe in the 'sinfulness of feeling happy' he fought the 1918 election against a Labour party that was determined to win over the discontented nonconformist vote. It was symbolic that Nicholls preached at Pool Wesley Chapel during the election campaign, while one of his principal supporters, W.G. Uglow, was to eventually commit the Camborne Divisional Labour Party to the virtually prohibitionist policy of closing ninety per cent of public houses in Cornwall.[142] This was probably a factor in the pro-Labour stance of C.V. Thomas in 1918 since he was a leading Wesleyan and had supported the wartime prohibition campaign. When Thomas welcomed Henderson to Camborne during the election he described him as 'a brother local preacher and a valued and honoured member in the Wesleyan Methodist Church'.[143] The danger for the Liberals was that Labour was starting to outflank the party on traditional issues just as much as on contemporary progressive concerns like internationalism and post-war reconstruction.

By 1922, however, the political landscape in Cornwall had been transformed. This was especially the case in the Mining Division where the Labour party could only poll just over a fifth of the vote in a three-cornered contest against both the Free Liberals and Coalition Liberals. The party was subsequently to remain in third place with only a quarter of the vote at best until 1945. Elsewhere, Labour struggled to make an impact, with only the party's slow but steady progress in Penryn & Falmouth providing some consolation. Part of the explanation lies with the collapse of the tin industry in Camborne after the war. Francis had assumed that he would receive the blame for the post-war problems of Cornish mining but the real loser was the Labour party since the onset of long-term unemployment undermined the trade unions, which in turn weakened local Labour party organisation.[144] Without a secure heartland the Labour movement was unable to capitalise on its initial progress and expand into the rural areas of the Duchy. The ability of Liberal candidates to take advantage of a changing political environment should not be ignored. Isaac Foot's victory in the Bodmin by-election in 1922 meant that Cornish Methodism now had a charismatic spokesman at Westminster. In the following year Leif

---

[141.] *Cornish Post,* 21 June 1917.
[142.] *Western Morning News,* 2 December 1918; *Royal Cornwall Gazette,* 20 October 1920.
[143.] *Cornish Post,* 14 December 1918.
[144.] *Royal Cornwall Gazette,* 22 November 1922; *West Briton,* 2 November 1922. For an account of the problems experienced by the local tin mining industry at this time see J. Rowe, 'The Declining Years of Cornish Tin Mining' in J. Porter (ed.), *Education and Labour in the South West,* Exeter, 1975, pp. 66 and 73.

Jones, who had won Camborne in a straight fight with a former Coalition Liberal, joined him in the House of Commons. Unlike Francis the new member for Camborne was well placed to appeal to local nonconformists since he was president of the United Kingdom Alliance, the leading temperance organisation, and son of a famous poet-preacher from Wales. This trend continued in the latter part of the decade when Maclean and Walter Runciman, another old-style Liberal, respected Methodist preacher and prohibitionist, contested the neighbouring divisions of North Cornwall and St Ives.[145]

The foundations were now laid for a remarkable resurgence in the cause of traditional Liberalism. Whilst Francis fought Hexham in 1929 as a committed supporter of Lloyd George's modernist agenda, the Cornish Liberals stressed issues relating to the core dynamics of the Duchy's provincial culture. Religious concerns from temperance to anti-Catholicism featured prominently during the 1929 election campaign, while economic issues were the need for free trade and lower taxation rather than the national pledge to conquer unemployment.[146] Following a landslide victory the five Liberal MPs then demonstrated their anti-metropolitan credentials by forming themselves into a new group entitled the Duchy Parliamentary Committee to co-ordinate their activities for both provincial and state affairs.[147] Significantly, the factors behind this recovery highlight the main arguments of Rokkan's model of centre-periphery politics. By exploiting the issues created by local cleavages it was possible to shift the focus away from the dominant political issues of the centre. Admittedly, new divisions within the Duchy Parliamentary Committee reflecting the wider problems of Liberalism throughout the United Kingdom were to usher in a new period of Conservative supremacy in Cornwall in the 1930s. But the crucial point was that Cornish Liberalism had been able to survive the 'Age of Alignment'. Liberal candidates were able to claim as a result that their party could 'understand Cornish folk and be in sympathy with their

---

145. In the late 1920s Walter Runciman was the leading exponent at the national level of the need for the Liberal party to project a distinctive image based on traditional policies like temperance. See Runciman papers, University of Newcastle, WR 219, Walter Runciman to Ilford Liberal Association, n.d. (c.1928); *Liberal Magazine,* Vol. 35, 1927, p. 219.
146. *Western Morning News,* 17 and 18 May 1929; Camborne Conservative Association papers, Cornwall Record Office, DDX/387/3, executive committee minutes, 21 October 1929; see also *Royal Cornwall Gazette,* 24 April, 15 May and 5 June 1929.
147. *Cornish Guardian,* 6 June 1929 and 16 January 1930; *Western Morning News,* 6 March 1930.

traditions and outlook on life'.[148] This anti-metropolitan stance was to be even more in evidence from the 1950s onwards as the party's early revival became associated with local issues ranging from economic marginalisation to political devolution.[149]

Such a solution for the problems of the Liberal party did not relate to the personal agenda of the Aclands. By 1929, however, their vision of the future had failed to become a reality. The dream of a new progressive force embracing Labour and the Liberals appeared no longer relevant since the former party looked set to continue a seemingly inevitable rise to power in its own right. Lloyd George's radical policy review of the late 1920s, a panacea that Francis had advocated with other radicals some ten years earlier, had simply come too late to reverse the realities of political realignment in urban Britain. Tentative moves in the late 1930s towards a Popular Front between Labour and the Liberals also came to an effective end with the onset of the Second World War. In conclusion it can be said that the importance of the Acland letters is the way in which they cover this drift into the political wilderness from the perspective of both high and low politics. The correspondence of Francis and Eleanor reveals their contribution to state politics during this critical period. Both individuals played an important if essentially neglected role in the campaign for female suffrage, the survival of independent Liberalism in the aftermath of the First World War and the events surrounding Lloyd George's radical crusade in the late 1920s. If Francis had been appointed as chairman of the Independent Liberals in 1919 it is conceivable that the nature of inter-war British politics might have developed somewhat differently. The letters also need to be considered in the context of provincial politics. Quite apart from providing a detailed record of constituency electioneering in the opening decades of the twentieth century, the collection offers new insight into the nature of politics outside Westminster. This is especially the case in Cornwall where the letters point to evidence of regional diversity ranging from the remarkably early challenge of Labour to the survival of an anti-metropolitan and nonconformist agenda that was to eventually result in the revival of Cornish Liberalism. By combining both macro and micro events this study therefore aims to enhance our understanding of British politics during the years after 1910 through the unifying perspective of a prominent Liberal family.

[148.] Penryn & Falmouth Conservative Association papers, Cornwall Record Office, DDX/551/11, electoral address of the Liberal candidate for Penryn & Falmouth in 1935.
[149.] *Cornish Guardian,* 8 May 1952 and 8 August 1957; *Cornish Times,* 15 and 22 August 1958; *New Cornwall,* Vol. 7, Issue 6, October–November 1959.

The Political Correspondence of Sir
Francis and Lady Acland, 1910–1929

Devon Record Office (DRO hereafter), 1148 M/511

FRANCIS ACLAND TO ELEANOR ACLAND

Holnicote[1], November 1910

I haven't found a touch of Liberalism anywhere yet. Men gaze & glower over the papers, & would curse Asquith[2] & applaud Lansdowne[3] if I weren't there.

I'm very glad about the pledge for the women[4] – & the Osborne judgement[5] – both on lines I like. Th'will be splendid if we win & can push things along a bit.

Even if the Tories win I think for very shame they'll have to make it more possible for Lib[eral] legislation to get through the Lords – but all that stiffness will come back & they'll try not to do anything that really matters.

I am sorry you won't be with me. We could have made it such a good time. . . . Uncle Charlie[6] is very wild about Ll[oyd] George's[7] remarks about aristocracy & I rather agree.

[1.] Holnicote, near Porlock, was the core of the Acland family estates in Somerset.
[2.] Herbert Henry Asquith (1852–1928) was Home Secretary 1892–95, Chancellor of the Exchequer 1905–08 and Prime Minister 1908–16. He was Liberal MP for East Fife 1886–1918 and Paisley 1920–24. Although ousted from the premiership in 1916, he remained the leader of the anti-Lloyd George Liberals. He led a reunited party (1923–26) and was created Earl of Oxford and Asquith in 1925
[3.] Henry Charles Keith Petty-Fitzmaurice (1845–1927) inherited the title of Marquis of Lansdowne in 1866. He was a Liberal junior minister 1869–74 and again in 1880. After resigning from the Liberals in 1880 he joined the Conservatives. He was Secretary for War 1895–1900, Foreign Secretary 1900–05, Minister without Portfolio 1915–16 and leader of the Unionists in the House of Lords 1903–16.
[4.] Presumably a reference to a speech by Asquith on 22 November which seemed to indicate that facilities would be provided for a suffrage bill if the Liberals were returned to office.
[5.] The Osborne judgement had removed the right of the trade unions to use funds for political purposes.
[6.] Sir Charles Thomas Dyke Acland (1842–1919) was the uncle of Francis and Liberal MP for East Cornwall and then North-East Cornwall 1882–92. He was appointed under secretary at the Board of Trade in 1886 and became the 12th baronet following the death of his father in 1898.
[7.] David Lloyd George (1863–1945) was Liberal MP for Carnarvon Boroughs 1890–1945 and Prime Minister 1916–22. He was President of the Board of Trade 1905–08, Chancellor of the Exchequer 1908–15, Minister of Munitions 1915–16, Secretary for War 1916 and leader of the Liberal party. In 1910 the Liberal campaign for the reform of the House of Lords led Lloyd George to make a number of provocative speeches against the power of the aristocracy.

DRO, 1148 M/512

FRANCIS ACLAND TO ELEANOR ACLAND

Liberal Committee Rooms, Camborne, 27 November 1910

Dearest,

Got your letter and the solemnities. I love to think of Cuthbert's[1] dark eyes roving around and him with his fist in his mouth.

All goes very well so far. I had nearly three hours yesterday afternoon with the Executive and the delegates and a meeting of 2500 afterwards winding up with a torchlight procession.

I am to be opposed by a Dr Coates[2] a man of about fifty who was at Balliol & fought Lichfield last time. That's all I know about him at present. Well, I really like the place and people so far. The Carkeeks[3] are quite a jolly family, though Mrs has not yet been visible being excitable & having been excited by the idea of the election, and therefore keeping quiet upstairs. There's a pleasant girl who acts hostess, engaged to the Lib[eral]. Sec[retary] for Redruth a most efficient looking young fellow, and a school-boy and school-girl – and a boy at Cambridge. And they live in an old highroomed house in ten acres of wood and garden & shrubbery.

I got on very well too with the President – a dentist with whom we took tea between the meetings. He's narrow minded but quite straight. His wife thinks women ratepayers should vote, but hasn't got further.

I read the Executive (25–30) my address & was well heckled over it. I didn't give complete satisfaction over right of entry on leasehold enfranchisement but luckily there were lots of other questions after that which I answered well – and brought them all around. Then upstairs to the delegates (300 or so) to whom I gave a brief autobiography and a general speech. This went very well and so did their questions.

I find the rumour is that I'm a high Churchman, and it was fun to deal with that. And there was an ex-Woolwich man who highly approved of me, and I got a chance of pleasing them about Bible teaching. Then a man asked would I stay as member beyond one Parliament – & I said it was a question of finance – and a young fellow got up & said he thought they ought to pay, & this was well received.[4]

When the fit and proper person resolution was put they kept popping up all over the hall to support it and I rammed it well in to them that they must work. Then I called the Executive again downstairs & made them appoint an advisory committee to meet every morning to see how things were going and to keep the agent up to his work.

At the evening meeting I was "statesmanlike" and got a tremendous lot into an hour and then come half a dozen really first rate short speeches in support, particularly from a Camborne man who is the biggest influence in the town, but kept out of the organisation because he's so big. He'd been on the other side till a few years ago, and came out tremendously strong for me. And then after great coaxing I got a few young Tories up to heckle and answered them most politely but much to the point, particularly "will you guarantee that Dr Coates shall get the same good treatment on Monday night". "If he gives the same satisfaction no doubt he'll get the same treatment" pleased them; and the whole thing ended with a forest of hands and great cheering for me, and you. Then quite unexpected & unbeknown to anyone the young Liberals had got up a torchlight procession and we had to walk round in an open carriage through the chief streets with a lot of hand song and cheering and jolly good fellowing. It was a great meeting from all over the division and will have done good & started people off well all round. If we can only keep the organisation up to the scratch everything will go splendidly.

[1.] Cuthbert Henry Dyke Acland (1910–79) was the youngest son of Francis and Eleanor. He subsequently became an agent for the National Trust in the Lake District.

[2.] Dr George Coates was born at Eccles near Manchester and educated at Derby and Balliol College, Oxford. He studied medicine in Germany and then practiced in London until 1903. He contested Lichfield as a Unionist in January 1910 and was then selected as the candidate for Camborne.

[3.] The Carkeeks lived at Penventon House, Redruth. Sir Arthur Carkeek (1861–1933) was a county councillor and businessman. He later became chairman of Camborne Liberal Association, Liberal parliamentary candidate for the neighbouring constituency of Penryn & Falmouth in 1918 and Chairman of Cornwall County Council 1931–33. His wife, Lady Carkeek (1862–1921), was a prominent local Methodist and vice-president of Camborne Liberal Association.

[4.] Salaries for MPs were introduced under the terms of the Parliament Act of 1911 and as a provision of that year's budget.

Bristol University Library (BUL hereafter), DM 668, National Liberal Club collection of election addresses

FRANCIS ACLAND TO THE ELECTORS OF CAMBORNE

Camborne, 1 December 1910

Gentlemen,

I have had the honour of being chosen by the Liberals of the Camborne or North-Western Division of Cornwall as their candidate in succession to

Mr Dunn,[1] whose retirement will, I believe be as much regretted by his friends and opponents here, as it is by his late colleagues in the House of Commons. And though it will be a difficult task to replace him at such short notice, no one who believes in democratic progress as I do can have any hesitation in coming forward.

Peers or People.

The dominating issue of this election is whether we shall or shall not, limit the power of the Lords to destroy democratic measures. In my opinion the Lords have too long blocked the forward path. We have asked them to pass the Parliament Bill which, while leaving them ample powers, would secure that the will of the people's representatives shall prevail without undue delay.[2] They have refused to pass it. They repent of nothing they have done, and merely produce illusory schemes for modifying the composition of their chamber, – schemes which would enable them with a greater show of decency to continue their evil work. *I stand, therefore, now for this principle: that the people shall govern themselves through those whom they elect, and that the absolute veto on progressive legislation claimed by the Lords shall be for ever done away.* This issue embraces all others. It is absolutely vital. If in this crisis we fail to secure *full* self-government, we shall lose all self-government, and we shall deserve to lose it. But if we succeed the way will be open before us to a long and splendid series of democratic reforms.

Licensing.

The way will be open for licensing legislation which shall on equitable terms give to the people the full control of the drink traffic in their own districts. This should include a provision for Sunday Closing.

Education.

The way will be open for giving the people full control of their own schools and for abolishing denominational tests upon the appointment of teachers. Only when these things are done can we hope to build up the educational system which we ought to have. Such a system can, in my opinion, include provisions allowing those who desire denominational religious instruction for their children to obtain it, but not at the public expense.

Ireland.

The way will be open for giving to Ireland, and I

hope also to each of the other parts of Great Britain, full control of its own local affairs. The case of Ireland is proved and should have priority. We have seen in South Africa how the grant of self-government has brought two hostile peoples into close friendship.[3] Can we not believe that generosity to Ireland (always maintaining in matters of common concern the supremacy of the House of Commons) will make all classes and creeds in that country, co-operate to secure its prosperity, in common loyalty to the British crown.

Disestablishment. The way will be open for Disestablishment of the Church in Wales.

Unemployment. The way will be open for removing the horrors of Unemployment, – by schemes of Insurance, by closing the blind alleys of boy labour, and by works of national development.

Electoral Reform. The way will be open for removing from wealth and prosperity the preponderating influence which they exercise in our politics. We must abolish the plural vote[4], reform registration, and open up the political career to all who can give good service to the State, by payment of Members of Parliament and of the necessary expenses of elections.

The way will be open for Adult Suffrage, under which every person over twenty-one years of age will have a vote. I believe that this will be the only permanently and finally satisfactory basis of self-government.

Poor Law. The way will be open for the reform of our Poor Law system. Now too often we only pauperise the destitute; – our aim should be to prevent destitution.

All the above-mentioned reforms I strongly support.

The Liberal Record I worked hard in the House of Commons to pass the Liberal legislation of the past four years, and I rejoice in the whole of it, for I believe it has brought help and hope and a chance of leading a better life to millions of our fellow-countrymen.

The Budget. I worked especially hard, as a Minister of the

Crown, in support of the Budget[5] of last year. I agreed with all its provisions and particularly welcomed the taxes on unearned increment and undeveloped value of urban land. Agricultural land is rightly exempted from this taxation.

The Fiscal Question. The more I see of the growing prosperity of England the more I believe in free trade. The more I see the world-wide struggle to throw off the yoke of trusts the more I hate Tariff Reform.

To pretend that Tariff Reform will give more employment is a fraud. It will certainly increase the prices of most of the ordinary necessities of life, and wages will never increase as much as the prices of the things they have to buy.

The Navy. I believe that we must maintain and have maintained the supreme strength of our navy, and I have every confidence that the present government will continue to maintain it.

The Army. I believe in voluntary support for our overseas Army and for Home Defence, and as Finance Member of the Army Council, I had ample opportunity of learning that compulsory military service would place a burden on our industry and our finances which is utterly unnecessary.

Imperial Policy. I believe that we should call the representatives of our great Dominions to take counsel with us on Imperial matters in an Imperial Senate. It is an insult to them to suggest that their loyalty depends upon our taxing for their benefit the necessary articles of the food of the people.[6]

On these and all other political matters I shall be glad to answer any questions which any elector may ask at any of my meetings. I hope that you will do me the honour of attending them, that you will conscientiously make up your minds after fairly considering the great issues placed before you, and that you will then record your votes, even at personal inconvenience, as your consciences dictate.

I trust that differences of political views will not stand in the way of my establishing personally friendly relations with my opponents. They will find if I am elected that I shall work for every one in the constituency to my utmost ability quite regardless of their political opinions.

I hope, therefore, that the contest may be friendly, and also that it may be short, so that Christmastide may not be disturbed and that it may bring to us all prosperity, peace and goodwill.

In each of the last three centuries members of my family have had the honour of representing Cornish seats in the House of Commons. It will be my constant endeavour that in this century also I may be found no less worthy than they of the trust and friendship of Cornishmen.

I am,

Your obedient servant,

Francis D. Acland

[1.] Albert Edward Dunn (1864–1937) came originally from Exeter and was Liberal MP for Camborne 1906–December 1910. He was on the Radical wing of the party and stood as the Labour candidate for the neighbouring seat of St Ives in 1918 and 1923.

[2.] A reference to what became the Parliament Act of 1911 which removed the right of the House of Lords to amend finance bills and its permanent veto of other bills passed by the House of Commons.

[3.] Refers to the Union of South Africa in 1910 which brought together the Dutch and British communities of the Cape of Good Hope, Natal, Orange Free State and Transvaal.

[4.] The plural vote refers to the system whereby businessmen were entitled to a second vote if their premises were located in a separate division to that of their residence.

[5.] This was Lloyd George's 'People's Budget' of 1909. Its rejection by the House of Lords had resulted in the constitutional crisis of 1910.

[6.] A criticism of the Unionist policy of imperial preference that was intended to bind Britain and the empire together through a preferential tariff scheme.

DRO, 1148 M/513

FRANCIS ACLAND TO ELEANOR ACLAND

Penventon, Redruth, December 1910

All goes <u>excellently</u>. I've got my last big open-air meeting capitally over. . . . I've written a letter to go out with the poll card. I've accomplished a big speech at Bodmin[1] 40 miles off. . . . It'll be all over now in a few days & I shall be in easily. The people simply love me. The hard lawyer impenetrable to sentiment says my speeches are hard high politics & nothing but politics – grand stuff. The emotional local preacher says they are the most stirring & uplifting things he's ever heard. So if I can please these two extremes I shall do all right.

I hope to get the same proportion as Dunn but there will be less votes both sides so the majority must be smaller. My friends will be disappointed if it's under 2000[2]. I shall be happy if it's over 1800. It's rather fun seeing the red & blue everywhere & hearing children yelling all the time as one goes about.

No one has said anything funny except one old man who looked as thick as a post. One of my speakers was describing the bribery in Falmouth, that a man had come to him & said he's got 10/– from the Tories as he went to dinner & 10/– from the Liberals as he came back & continued "now what should you do if you were exposed to temptations of that kind". And the old boy spoke "I should go to dennerr again".

"Up Acland" is the popular cry and "That's the colour" when they see the red & blue.

Things seem to go fairly in the world outside but we have all the worst of the luck.

[1] This speech was outside his constituency and presumably in support of Isaac Foot, the Liberal candidate for Bodmin.
[2] In the event Francis obtained a majority of 2,093 votes in a straight fight with the Unionists. He polled 4,419 votes compared to 2,326 for his opponent.

DRO, 1148 M/516

FRANCIS ACLAND TO ELEANOR ACLAND

Bassett Road Villas, Camborne, December 1910

Dearest,

I have missed post & shall not post this till tomorrow but it will make me feel less lonesome to write to you. I am being well treated, but am spending most of the day with a prominent solicitor, [a] Wesleyan, who has a pleasant family & a large and comfortable house.

. . . I am really getting towards the end and things are going well enough. I was glad of the 3 Liberal gains for people to read of in their Sunday morning papers but the counties are not doing so well as I hoped and I fear very much for Torquay & Bodmin.[1] I think the truth must be that in the nonconformist districts where we would expect things to perk up because of the lessened Tory pressure and work, people have been so thoroughly worked up by religious bigotry against Home Rule that things have come out about all square.

I have 6 meetings tomorrow but only three on each of the next days, and after that I can sit still and do nothing if I like.

We shall lose a lot of votes through having no cars, and many of our supporters won't run traps[2] unless they are paid but if it's a fine day there is still a possibility of a majority of over 2000.

At last the weather looks better & there's only been a little rain today & we actually had two meetings out of three last night without rain – & splendid audiences accordingly.

I have much more voice than ever before on a Sunday.

[1] Both Torquay and Bodmin were lost to the Conservatives by 130 and 41 votes respectively.

[2] Candidates were dependent on their wealthier supporters for traps and cars to convey electors to polling stations. This tended to give the advantage to the Unionists. See Henry Pelling, *Social Geography of British Elections 1885–1910*, Macmillan, 1967, p. 12.

DRO, 1148 M/514

FRANCIS ACLAND TO ELEANOR ACLAND

14 December 1910

I am still very fit and am acclaimed as a "most magnificent orator". It is very difficult to know what is going to happen – as our organisation is ridiculous – (lots of my addresses not yet delivered!), and I can't find out how much the anti-Catholic rant is affecting the nonconformists. I take things very easy & don't do anything except meetings – & all meetings go splendidly – as they did in Richmond –

The Tories are not working & don't put any heart into the fight, but as you know they always vote.

We lost two seats in the West[1] as you saw – which will affect things here – & if we lose Truro Helston[2] today things would really drop away a good deal. I don't think we shall lose there though – & I can't think that even if we do our majority will fall below 1500.

I think 1800 probable & 2000 possible – but we shall see.

[1] Refers to the loss of both Bodmin and Torquay to the Unionists.

[2] George Hay-Morgan, the Liberal MP for Truro-Helston 1906–18, eventually retained the seat but his majority fell from 611 to 397.

Cornubian, 22/12/10

FRANCIS ACLAND TO THE ELECTORS OF THE CAMBORNE DIVISION

December 1910

Gentlemen,

I very highly appreciate the proud position in which you have placed me. It will be my constant endeavour to justify the choice which you have made. I desire to thank all who have during this contest rendered service to the Liberal cause. Splendid work has been done on all sides to keep the flag of Liberalism flying. To all my constituents, regardless of party, my thanks are due for the friendly spirit in which this election has been conducted.

I shall try to do my duty, to the best of my ability, for everyone regardless of the party to which he may belong.

May I conclude by wishing you all a united and Merry Christmas and prosperous New Year.

Yours faithfully,

F.D. Acland

DRO, 1148 M/24

HERBERT ASQUITH TO FRANCIS ACLAND

10, Downing Street, London, 30 January 1911

My dear Acland,

It would be a great pleasure to me, and a real service to the Government, if you could see your way to resume your old place as Financial Secretary at the War Office.

Yours sincerely,

H.H.Asquith

DRO, 1148 M/518

FRANCIS ACLAND TO ELEANOR ACLAND

October 1911

Damn, Damn & ten thousand times Damn. Look at this! What could I do? I got it at 9.15 & had to write at once.[1] So I said "my heart is all in home politics but of course I should be glad to work for Grey[2] and must leave myself in Asquith's hands. I don't speak French". Of the whole tribe of useless worms on this earth I think diplomats are the worst. But I feel on telegraphing & still feel that if I'm not thought worthy of any of the more important home jobs – and its just a case of taking this or staying where I am I'd better take it, though its not a step up at all that I can see.

Its rotten bad luck not having had any notice that changes were on, and having no real chance to see what arrangements might have been possible.

Things go to the pushers and not to the waiters, and though I know I could run Education or Agriculture or the F[inancial]. Sec[retary]ship to the Treasury well I suppose I really haven't done enough work that anyone knows about to have a real claim to any of these.

And so having got into one corner I go to another corner which is only just less hard to get out of than the one I was in before.

[1.] This letter reveals Francis's annoyance at being offered the post of Under Secretary of State at the Foreign Office under Sir Edward Grey when he much preferred an appointment with one of the domestic ministries. He eventually accepted the offer.

[2.] Sir Edward Grey (1862–1933) was Foreign Secretary 1905–16. He was first elected to Parliament in 1892 as Liberal MP for Berwick-on-Tweed and was under secretary of state for Foreign Affairs 1892–95. In 1916 he became Viscount Grey of Falloden and Liberal leader in the House of Lords 1923–24.

DRO, 1148 M/527

FRANCIS ACLAND TO ELEANOR ACLAND

October 1911?

Reflection brings a calmer mood but I'm not happy about the proposed change though I think I really prefer it to staying where I am. Whatever happens however I shall not mind or rejoice much. It was odd that in my agitation I made the two best speeches I've ever made yesterday; but it really was bad luck that I was away here with no time to think, & no knowledge to guide me.

Don't lock the doors I may turn up in the night or early morning. We have no Sunday papers so I don't know whether the moves are 'out'. It's a tantalising time to 'wait and see'.[1]

[1.] Presumably echoing Asquith's famous use of the phrase 'wait and see' in relation to the Parliament Act Procedure Bill in 1910. See David Butler and Anne Sloman, *British Political Facts 1900–1979*, Macmillan, 5th edition, 1980, p. 247.

Cornubian, 31/10/12

FRANCIS ACLAND TO THE EDITOR OF 'THE CORNUBIAN'

House of Commons, 25 October 1912

Sir,

I should be very much obliged if you will allow me to use your columns for explaining to my constituents how they can best secure admission to the House of Commons to hear debates on their visits to London. When visitors come from so far one is particularly desirous that they should be able to see and hear all that is possible.

But not infrequently a card is sent in to me by someone desiring admission without any previous notice of his visit. Then it sometimes happens that I am attending some meeting in Committee outside the House or am engaged at the Foreign Office, and am unable to come, but more frequently I am on the spot but quite unable at such short notice to secure tickets of admission. We secure these tickets by balloting a week ahead. I secure tickets about once out of four times I ballot for them. But even when I do not succeed in the ballot I can generally get tickets if I know they will be wanted by going at once to those who have secured them, whose names are exhibited daily on a list, and asking for their tickets if they do not want them particularly. But one cannot do this with any success if one does not know of any intended visit until one or two days before the visit, or on the day itself, for one then finds that all tickets have been disposed of.

If, therefore visitors from the Mining Division[1] will let me know the days on which they would like to visit the House, at least a week before the date of visit, giving me an address in London to which the tickets can be sent, I can generally oblige them, or will always do my best to do so; regardless, of course, of the politics or sex of the visitor.

But if persons come without notice they will find that tickets are impossible to obtain or that the galleries are absolutely full, and I shall be as disappointed as they will be at their ill fortune.

Yours faithfully,

F.D. Acland

[1.] The local importance of mining in the Camborne/Redruth area ensured that this was the popular name given to the Camborne division.

Bodleian Library, Asquith papers, MS. Asquith 13, fols 89. 89a–c

FRANCIS ACLAND TO ERIC DRUMMOND[1]

5 Cheyne Place, London, November 1912

Dear Drummond,

Would you let the P.M. have the enclosed, or the substance of it.

Yours most truly,

F.D. Acland

The P.M. should be informed upon a technical point in connection with women suffrage. To give women the vote "on the same terms as men" is not to give them the vote "on a democratic basis" under our present Registration Laws. As to owners & lodgers the law would not equally and similar classes of men and women would be enfranchised in these classes under "equal terms". But the vast bulk of male voters are occupiers and for the franchise to be broad and democratic the ordinary voter's wife or other female relation resident with him in the same tenement should be enfranchised. But the removal of the sex disqualification would not secure this under our present law. She could only come on the register as a "joint occupier" and joint occupation can only be obtained if the tenement be of over £20 annual value, and by consent of the present occupier, and of the landlord. Practically all working men occupy tenements of under £20 annual value, so all their wives would be "automatically disenfranchised", and the middle and upper class wife or other female relations could obtain the vote only if the male occupier applied to the landlord for the woman's name to be put into the agreement of tenancy, and if the landlord were willing. So "equal terms" really means (except for owners & lodgers) a middle and upper class landlord male vote so long as the present franchise remains as it is for men. This is the franchise that Lord R[obert]. Cecil[2] has been advocating at the annual Conservative Caucus meetings – explaining that it would enable the Liberals to be permanently excluded from office. Of course under the Gov[ernmen]t's proposals for a brief residential qualification the difficulty would disappear, and "equal terms" & "a broad democratic basis" would mean the same thing, – but they don't mean the same thing now. I write this note in the hope that the P.M. will see further suffrage deputations. It does them good – and may do him good!

[1.] James Eric Drummond (1876–1951) was Asquith's private secretary 1912–15. He was a civil servant at the Foreign Office 1915–19 and served as the first secretary general of the League of Nations 1919–33 before becoming the British Ambassador to Italy 1933–39. In 1937 he became the seventh Earl of Perth and in 1946 became deputy leader of the Liberal party in the House of Lords.

[2.] Lord Robert Cecil (1864–1958) was Conservative MP for Hertfordshire 1911–23. He was appointed Under Secretary at the Foreign Office in 1915 and was Lord Privy Seal 1923–24 and Chancellor of the Duchy of Lancaster 1924–27. Became Viscount Chelwood in 1923.

DRO, 1148 M/25

EDWARD GREY TO FRANCIS ACLAND

Falloch, 26 December 1912

My dear Francis,

All good wishes to you & your wife & the children for the coming year & thank you very much for your letter.

You deal very well with all the things in the House of Commons & in the Office & it is a great relief to me to feel that they are in such safe hands & I am grateful though I haven't much time to express it.

We aren't out of the wood yet about Balkan affairs,[1] but I think we are through the most impenetrable thicket. I am optimistic.

There has been no setback in the news since I left London: of course there is a lot of work. I had 3 solid hours on Christmas morning and nearly another hour before tea to get the stuff back to London; but I have enjoyed my four days here.

Yours sincerely,

E. Grey

1. The Balkan Wars of 1912–13 created the instability in Eastern Europe that led to the outbreak of the First World War. In 1912 Bulgaria, Greece, Montenegro and Serbia captured much of the European territories of the Ottoman Empire but in the following year a new war started between Bulgaria and Serbia.

DRO, 1148 M/523

FRANCIS ACLAND TO ELEANOR ACLAND

1913?

Look at Mckenna's[1] answer on the Piccadilly Flat[2] case today. It explodes whole clouds of rumours. He told me that when he did see the list of the frequenters the only name he knew was one of a committee which [?] has formed to expose Liberal iniquities.

I have to make a speech at a lunch on Thursday to all the swell foreign doctors at the lunch which my medical school is giving them. And later on Thursday I have to speak on opium. It is the Indian budget night & the opium people have got the motion on going into committee. Montagu[3] has to lead off & speak for two hours & to wind up – so he's asked me to take opium which will come on in the middle. . . . Dickinson[4] thinks & I agree with him that we must launch a Liberal Suff[rage]. Soc[iety] in the Autumn & that that's the way to do literature etc. We are to talk it over with Grey. It will be closely parallel to yours in policy, but with Grey President and all the Suff[rage] ministers Vice Presidents etc. I hope it will come off.

1. Reginald McKenna (1863–1943) was Liberal MP for North Monmouthshire 1895–1918 and Home Secretary at the time when this letter was written. He was Financial Secretary to the Treasury 1905–07, President of the Board of Education 1907–08, First Lord of the Admiralty 1908–11, Home Secretary 1911–15 and Chancellor of the Exchequer 1915–16.
2. In July 1913 a London prostitute, named Queenie Gerald, was convicted of running a brothel in her flat in Piccadilly. There were allegations that some of Gerald's wealthy customers included a number of prominent Liberals and that McKenna as Home Secretary had prevented a list of their names from being revealed to the public.
3. Edwin Samuel Montagu (1879–1924) was Liberal MP for Chesterton 1906–18 and Coalition Liberal MP for Cambridgeshire 1918–22. He was Parliamentary under-secretary at the India Office 1910–14, Financial Secretary to the Treasury 1914–15 & 1915–16, Chancellor of the Duchy of Lancaster 1915 & 1916, Minister of Munitions 1916 and Secretary of State for India 1917–22.

4. Sir Willoughby Hyett Dickinson (1859–1943) was Liberal MP for St Pancras North 1906–18 and a prominent campaigner for female suffrage. In 1913 he had introduced a Women's Suffrage Bill to the House of Commons but this was defeated by 269 to 221 votes.

National Archives, Kew, HO 45/10710/242402

J.F. WILLIAMS TO FRANCIS ACLAND

Lamledra, Gorran Haven, 2 September 1913

Dear Acland:-

I hope you will forgive my writing to you when you are probably on a holiday or what is for a Cornish M.P. a matter of business, but I have been watching the China Clay strike[1] with some interest and should like to write a line or two as to the handling of the police – a subject on which probably more will be heard in the future.

The Chief Constable of Cornwall[2] has issued a proclamation or "Police Warning" in which he commits himself to the curiously vague statement that "anything in the nature of" unlawful assembly is punishable, and he goes on to quote two definitions of unlawful assembly given by two learned judges – which like many other legal utterances are both discordant and obscure. The result is that at present in the St Austell district wherever four or five strikers are gathered together ("meetings" of three are permitted) in circumstances which seem to the policemen on the spot (often imported from South Wales[3]) suspicious, the police lay on with their batons and "disperse the mob". Let me enclose you a cutting from to-day's Daily Mercury in support of this – a cutting giving the Police Version of the affair. You will see that it is plain that the police attacked.

I went round most of the clay district this afternoon in a motor. There were policemen everywhere. The whole place had a Russian appearance. Groups of men were on the peaks of the St Austell Alps like the chamois in Cook's pictures of Switzerland. The district is quiet – terrorised into quiet. But the whole countryside is full of rumours; this morning in our little fishing village – and we have no connection with the strikers – over 11 miles away – there was a rumour that a man and a little girl had been killed by the Welsh strike-breakers – and things were said not pleasant for a Liberal to hear. The truth is that the police – good-natured civil enough men in their way – look on the strikers as natural enemies and jump at any occasion of hammering them with batons – not such a difficult task for athletic well-fed policemen.

Now I don't write this merely in the air, but with a view to suggesting that there ought to be some sort of general rule enforced on the police during strikes, and it ought not to be open to a Chief Constable to issue the sort of proclamation that the Chief Constable of Cornwall has signed. (It may be that the proclamation is the work of the Home Office – if so, the matter is even more serious).

The strikers in this case are in my judgement right – though this is really irrelevant – on the main issue. They want their union recognised and I think that over here general opinion supports them in this. But right or wrong they ought to be handled more legally than is the case now. Incidents such as yesterday's make them feel themselves outcasts, with all society fighting against them. But rightly handled they are no such desperadoes: their meeting last night ended with "Lead, kindly Light" and the Benediction.[4]

Yours sincerely,

J.F. Williams

[1.] The Cornish Clay Strike in the summer of 1913 was the result of a campaign for union recognition and higher pay. In the event the strikers were unsuccessful and were forced back to work in the autumn.

[2.] A reference to Lieutenant Colonel Hugh Protheroe-Smith who was Chief Constable of the Cornwall Police Constabulary 1909–35. He had a distinguished military career that included the Sudan campaign in 1898 and received a knighthood in 1928.

[3.] The Welsh police units from South Glamorgan had experience of controlling industrial disputes, particularly in the coal mining areas of South Wales.

[4.] Hymns and bible readings featured prominently at the meetings of the clay strikers. One of the leading figures in the strike movement was the Rev. Booth Coventry, a Methodist minister.

National Archives, HO 45/10710/242402

J.F.WILLIAMS TO FRANCIS ACLAND

Lamledra, Gorran Haven, Cornwall, 14 September 1913

Dear Acland:-

Many thanks for your letter. Since the trouble on the 1st September things have been reasonably quiet and peaceful picketing has not been interfered with. There are however signs that the men are feeling the strain of the strike and I should not now be surprised any day to hear of violence that puts them hopelessly on the wrong side of the law.

I enclose you a letter of mine in this week's Nation: the latter part is in the nature of speculation and need not detain you – what is in the back of my mind is that in the future "blacklegging" will probably be made impossible among working men as it is among our professionals – partly by the pressure of social opinion and partly by law – and in the meantime I personally should deprecate taking too much trouble to smooth the way for blacklegs or strike breakers at any rate in cases where no violence has been done. In the same way I should not be anxious to help a landlord to close all accustomed (but not legal) accesses to such beautiful places as these cliffs here. But this is not the practical politics of the moment.

What is important at the moment is some general rule for the application of the difficult doctrine of "unlawful assembly". Would it be impossible for the Home Office to draft confidentially a sort of "model proclamation" for the use of Chief Constables at the outbreak of a strike? I don't know, writing away from books, what is the authority for the Definition of Unlawful Assembly that I refer to in my letter to the Nation as not altogether satisfactory: the Chief Constable's proclamation says "One of His Majesty's judges" – and D.D. Robertson to whom I wrote could not identify the reference: you will see that the Judge whoever he is, simply says "other persons" where Archbold says "firm and courageous persons in the neighbourhood of the assembly", and the Chief Constable's other authority requires "circumstances of terror". I enclose you an extract from the Chief Constable's proclamation and a note sent me by D.D. Robertson. Do not trouble to return them.

Yours,

J.F. Williams

Extract from Proclamation by the Chief Constable of Cornwall during the China Clay Strike of August and September 1913

Police Warning

Malicious Damage to Property and Unlawful Assembly. (quotes 24 and 25 Vict. c.97. s.52 – wilful damage to property).

Peaceful picketing is lawful in trade disputes but anything in the nature of unlawful assembly is punishable.

An unlawful assembly has been defined by one of His Majesty's Judges as a meeting "which attempted to carry out any common purpose lawful or unlawful in such a manner as to give other persons reason to fear a disturbance of the peace".

It has also been laid down that any meeting whatever of great numbers of people with such circumstances of terror as cannot but endanger the public peace or create alarm among persons of reasonable firmness and courage is unlawful.

National Archives, HO 45/10710/24202

FRANCIS ACLAND TO J.F. WILLIAMS

Foreign Office, London, 22 October 1913

Sir,

I am directed by the Secretary of State to say that he has had under his careful consideration your letter of the 17th ultimo with enclosures relating to the warning against taking part in unlawful assemblies which was issued to the Public last August by the Chief Constable of Cornwall. The poster in question was issued by the Chief Constable in the exercise of his own discretion, and without previous consultation with the Home Office: and, although it does not contain such a precise statement of the law as would be necessary in a criminal code or legal text book, the Secretary of State has no reason to think that it has led the police to exceed their powers in the maintenance of order – or prevented the Strikers from the proper exercise of any legal right. The Secretary of State is not responsible for the notices which Local Police Authorities may find it desirable to issue from time to time but he will consider whether it is possible to prepare any model form of notice which they might be advised to use when occasion requires. It will not however be easy to find a form of words which will convey precisely the effect of all the decided cases on the question of what constitutes an unlawful meeting – and at the same time be so plain in its terms as to be understood by the ordinary citizen and so brief and impressive as to serve effectively as a warning.

I am,
Sir,
Your obedient Servant

––––––––––

BUL, DM 1193, *Women's Liberal Federation News*, Vol. IV, No. 11, 1 November 1913.

ELEANOR ACLAND TO THE EDITOR OF THE 'WOMEN'S LIBERAL FEDERATION NEWS'

29, Denison House, Vauxhall Bridge Road, S.W., October 1913

Dear Madam,

Most of your readers will have in their hands recently two leaflets containing each a different selection of extracts from one article by Mr. Lloyd George, an article in the July number of *Nash's Magazine* on the present Position of Woman Suffrage.

One of these leaflets, published by the W[omen's]. L[iberal]. F[ederation]., contains the views expressed by Mr. Lloyd George on the general aspect of the question. Liberal women must be glad to read therein that the Chancellor of the Exchequer is now firmer than ever in supporting Woman Suffrage as a necessary consequence of the increasing influence of the State over women's lives and concerns.[1] We must note too, as of vital importance, Mr Lloyd George's declaration that "no franchise bill can ever be brought forward in this country without raising the whole problem of whether you are going to exclude more than half the citizens of the land", *i.e.*, the women.

The other leaflet gives chiefly such extracts from the same article by Mr. Lloyd George as refer to militancy, its disastrous consequences and the best means of combating these.

We all agree that militancy, in its later phases at any rate, has created an atmosphere unfavourable to the grant of Woman Suffrage; this is because militancy has made the Woman Suffrage movement appear to be one of sex-antagonism, whereas it is really one of sex-comradeship.[2] But many of us may find it impossible to agree with Mr. Lloyd George when he says that: "If they (the militants) had accepted Mr. Asquith's pledge of November, 1911, Woman Suffrage would by now have been an accomplished fact". How? Mr. Lloyd George himself declared that the plan of November, 1911 (the plan that is of putting women into a Reform Bill by means of a free vote on a non-party amendment) had torpedoed the Conciliation Bill plan. But surely it was the Speaker's Ruling in January, 1913, which torpedoed the new plan that had torpedoed an old plan!

Be that as it may, my real object in writing to you, Madam, now is to call your readers' special attention to the final paragraph quoted in this leaflet on militancy–the paragraph which deals with the question: "What is to be done now to combat the ill-effects of militancy?" Mr Lloyd George asks for a *new movement*.

What can be the nature of this new movement? Is it to be non-party? But of non-party constitutional agitation we have had no lack. Personally I believe that the time for non-party action, either by women or by friends of woman suffrage in Parliament, has gone by; and that it is time for the women of that party which provides the bulk of suffragist Members of Parliament (*i.e.*, the Liberal Party) to make a great stand for the principle that the Liberal ideal of self-government must apply to women as well as to men. That is why the Liberal Women's Suffrage Union has been inaugurated.[3] We want to prove that Liberal women are, in Mr. Lloyd George's own words, "Sane, hard-headed and practical." We want to prove that we are in earnest. It does not seem to me that Liberal women who go "on strike", that is adopt an anti-Government policy, are doing the wisest thing, and I still think we ought to prove our faith in the Liberal Party, and in the suffragists who are in powerful positions in that Party. Therefore I believe in the policy of the new Liberal Women's Suffrage Union–the simple policy of supporting Liberal suffragist candidates, and Liberal suffragist candidates only. By so doing we prove our own sincerity, and until we have done that we must expect some insincerity on the part of men. So long as we put the claims of justice to women below the exigencies of immediate party success men will do the same. But that is not the sort of action, the sort of idea, that has brought the Liberal Party to the proud position it now holds, *nor that can keep it there.*

This new movement of ours is a suffrage movement; but it is also a Liberal movement. Its success depends upon how much sane, hard-headed sincerity Liberal women can muster. It may be well to add that already, though our work as a Society is hardly started, Liberal Suffrage men in various parts of the country are beginning to recognise it and to turn their minds to the question of the formation of a Liberal Suffragist Society for men also. For my part I believe we shall see important developments in this direction before the General Election, if we ourselves can only make the effort to set an example.

Yours sincerely,
ELEANOR ACLAND,
Hon. Secretary,
Liberal Women's Suffrage Union

[1.] The Liberal cabinet was divided on the issue of women's suffrage. Asquith in particular was opposed to reform. However, Lloyd George was seen as more sympathetic and regarded as a pivotal figure in any moves to introduce female suffrage.

[2.] Militant action tended to be associated with the Women's Social and Political Union (WSPU) which had been established in 1903 by Emmeline Pankhurst (1858–1928). Their pre-war campaign to win the right to vote included chaining themselves to railings and hunger strikes in prison.

[3.] It appears that Eleanor was the driving force in the creation of the Liberal Women's Suffrage Union. By the end of the year the LWSU was being described as 'Mrs. Acland's society'. See Jo Vellacott, *From Liberal to Labour with Women's Suffrage: The Story of Catherine Marshall,* McGill – Queen's University Press, 1993, pp. 228–9 and 279

Cornubian, 12/02/14

FRANCIS ACLAND TO THE EDITOR OF
'THE CORNUBIAN'

February 1914

Sir,

I have been reading Lord Ampthill's[1] recent speech at Camborne. In view of the undoubted seriousness of the Irish question it is our duty to examine the suggestion which he made whereby rebellion in Ulster could be avoided.[2] He says it can be avoided by a general election. May I respectfully ask Unionists who may be inclined to agree with to consider a few questions.

1. Did not Lord Lansdowne say before the last election that Mr Asquith had made it perfectly clear that he intended to use the parliament Act to pass Home Rule? If he did why should we be bound to have another election before carrying out our clearly expressed intention?

2. If there were such an election are Unionists willing to make it, so far as they can, a test of our feelings on the Irish question by pledging themselves not to use a majority, if they obtained one, for starting Tariff Reform, or making the Insurance Act[3] voluntary (i.e. destroying it), or repealing the Parliament Act? If not, is it not rather nonsense for them to pretend that they wish for a general election to settle the Irish question only?

3. Even if there were an election on this issue have the Ulster leaders ever said that they would pay any attention to its result? Have they not, on the contrary, always said that whatever the result of our elections they would always refuse to allow their country to manage its own internal affairs for itself? If this is so, are they not just as likely to make a rebellion after an election as they are without one?

With all possible respect to Lord Ampthill's suggestion, I fear that it needs a great deal more consideration than he seems to have given it, and that the more it is considered the clearer it becomes that another general election would not settle the Ulster difficulty in the least.

Yours faithfully,

F.D. Acland

---

[1] Arthur Oliver Villers Russell (1869–1935) had been appointed assistant secretary at the Colonial Office in 1895 and was Governor of Madras 1900–06. He had inherited the title of Baron Ampthill in 1884.

2. Dependent on support from the Irish Nationalists the Liberals had introduced an Irish Home Rule bill in 1912. Many Ulster Protestants refused to accept rule from Dublin and they were supported by the Unionists in Britain. The formation of the Ulster Volunteer Force in 1913 meant that by the eve of the First World War the island appeared to be on the verge of civil war.

3. The National Insurance Act of 1911 provided limited unemployment benefit for manual workers in certain industries subject to recurrent unemployment. The scheme was financed by a compulsory weekly levy from the government, employers and employees.

ELEANOR ACLAND TO THE EDITOR OF THE 'WESTERN MORNING NEWS'

5, Cheyne Place, S.W. London, 26 June 1914

Sir,

I should be very much obliged if you would publish the enclosed letter to Miss Mattieson, Honorary Secretary of the South-Western Federation of the National Union of Women's Suffrage Societies[1] as I desire that my position towards the Liberal party may be perfectly clear to Liberal Suffragists in the West.

As an ardent Suffragist, and Liberal I am convinced that if the Liberal party put Women's Suffrage on their next programme they will not only be doing a splendid act of justice, but will also immensely strengthen their hold over the minds and hearts of many true lovers of liberty. Many such people are growing more and more discontented at the way in which women's claim to self-government is continually ignored by the party which has always stood for self-government.

Therefore, with the object of uniting the Liberal party on the question of Women's Suffrage, our Liberal Women's Suffrage Union is urging Liberal women to work more energetically than ever for Liberal Suffragist candidates and to refrain from doing political work for Liberals who deny their political capacity.

Eleanor Acland

(copy.)

Dear Miss Mattieson,

I have been for some time considering my position as Vice-President of the South-West Federation of the National Union of Women's Suffrage Societies, and I have reluctantly come to the conclusion that that position is incompatible with my position on the Liberal Women's Suffrage Union. I am therefore obliged to ask you to tender my resignation to your Committee. I will give my reasons briefly, as follows:

1. The N.U.W.S.S. does not allow any member of a local committee to support any Liberal candidate, even though he be a declared Suffragist, and even if there be no N.U.W.S.S. candidate in the field. I hear from Liberal women at Grimsby and Ipswich that as they have supported the Liberals there they have been requested to resign their posts on the local Executive of those branches. This is the more unfair, in that apparently no objection is taken to Conservative women in a similar position supporting the Conservative candidate.

2. Further, I am opposed to the policy of putting up third candidates, or helping to do so, where the Liberal candidate is a Suffragist.[2] I cannot see that the Labour party has at present sacrificed anything for the suffrage. They, rightly or wrongly, equally with the Radical Suffragist group, support the present Government, and most of them voted for the abolition of Plural Voting Bill.

3. I am convinced that the present policy of the N.U.W.S.S. is alienating Liberals and I find that my position as vice president of your Federation makes the work I am trying to do among Liberals open to misunderstanding.

As to the refusal of Liberal candidates to receive deputations from your Society I cannot see what inducement you offer them to do so, seeing that whatever pledges they give you, you are debarred by the policy of the N.U.W.S.S. from giving them any support.

I am aware that the present policy of the N.U.W.S.S. was only maintained by a very narrow majority at the last Conference and as a Liberal woman I feel it my duty to use whatever influence I have towards getting that policy modified.

I propose to send a copy of this letter to the editor of 'The Western Daily Mercury'.

Yours sincerely,
Eleanor Acland

---

[1] The National Union of Women's Suffrage Societies (NUWSS) was established in 1897. It advocated a non-militant approach to obtaining parliamentary suffrage for women on the same lines as men.

[2] In 1912 the NUWSS had formed the Election Fighting Fund Committee. The aim of this committee was to put pressure on the Liberal government by providing financial support and general assistance for Labour candidates. This threatened the ostensibly non-party nature of the NUWSS and caused a particular dilemma for Liberals like Eleanor.

DRO, 1148 M/874

RONALD ROSS TO ELEANOR ACLAND

28 June 1914

Dear Mrs Acland,

Very many thanks for your letter. The great difficulty that faces everyone in England in this question is the impossibility of judging Irish politics by English standards. You can't judge our tribal warfare by the pleasant English game. To be governed by the Nationalist majority is <u>destruction</u> for us & not merely a question akin to 1d in the pound extra for wealthy manufacturers. We always said we would go down fighting it & so we will. I believe that Liberal opinion in England is at last realizing this & it is the fault of their leaders that they did not do so before. The amazing lack of insight of Ll[oyd]. G[eorge] saying it is aristocratic business shows how out of touch he & the rest have got. They cannot understand a point so overwhelming as to unite an entire community irrespective of class.

How a party which calls itself progressive can hand over a body of efficient people to the blighting influences of a Nationalist government I can't understand.

As to what that influence is I only ask you to read the report of any mixed deputation that has been over here. Of course I have been told a thousand times that with responsibility this will alter but I have never heard this from anyone but optimistic English Liberals who know nothing of Ireland.

If you think the rest of Ireland are as keen for H[ome]. R[ule]. as we are against it you make a big mistake. I suspect you consider my opinion on this point worthless but I have seen a good deal of the south having been born outside Ulster & lived longer out of Ulster than in it.

BUL, DM 1193, *Women's Liberal Federation News,* Vol. V, No. 7, 1 July 1914

ELEANOR ACLAND TO THE WOMEN'S LIBERAL FEDERATION NEWS

June 1914?

DEAR MADAM,

It was my intention to ask for urgency for the following resolution at the Council meetings:

"That this Council expresses its cordial appreciation of the action of the Scottish and Welsh Liberal members in providing for the inclusion of women in the proposed electorate for the Local Parliaments of Scotland and Wales".[1]

But much time was spent on our Suffrage debates and we already had one necessary appeal for "Urgency" in connection with the recent increase in militant outrages. And I know that appeals for "Urgency" are not popular with delegates. I therefore felt that it would be more effective if as many individual W[omen]. L[iberal]. A[ssociation].s as possible would carry resolutions to the above effect and send them by post to the Secretaries of the Scottish and Welsh Liberal Members' Committee, House of Commons, Westminster.

I most earnestly appeal to all Honorary Secretaries to take action on these lines, because it would be a great pity if this act of justice appeared to be overlooked by Women Liberals.

Yours sincerely,
ELEANOR ACLAND

[1.] By 1914 female suffrage campaigners within the Liberal party saw the campaign for Scottish and Welsh devolution as an opportunity to advance their cause. This was particularly the case in regard to the Scottish Home Rule Bill in May of that year.

Cornubian, 06/08/14

FRANCIS ACLAND TO THE EDITOR OF 'THE CORNUBIAN'

Foreign Office, London, 4 August 1914

Dear Sir,

The question whether the policy of the government should be supported by all good citizens is one of the utmost gravity.[1] It cannot be lightly decided by our feelings of affection or dislike for particular countries. Neither can we say, however much we love peace or love war, that peace or war at all costs is a clear and imperative necessity. We must know the sequence of events which has led to this great catastrophe, we must study what are our obligations and interests therein. It would have been my duty and desire by speaking to my constituents to give them what guidance I could in forming a right judgement. But every person in the service of the Crown has his post and must remain there, and as long as I can be of use at the Foreign Office I must stay there. But I hope to be able to communicate a statement to my constituents through the Press as soon as the full materials for forming a complete judgement are available.

Meanwhile may I venture to state to them what seems to me to be the duty of all good citizens. There is financial security, and our food supplies are safe, so they should not try to withdraw money from the banks, or buy food to greater quantity than they need. The most dangerous prospect before us is one of widespread unemployment due to the restriction of our foreign trade, and this is certain whether the United Kingdom be at peace or at war with Foreign Powers. Therefore all we can afford to keep in their employment those whom they usually employ should do so as a high patriotic duty. And those who lose employment should be helped by all who can afford to help them. "Be ye brethren one towards another" is the Devine word which should now and henceforth guide our actions.

Yours faithfully,

F.D. Acland

[1.] The outbreak of the First World War caused particular problems for those Liberals on the left of the party. Charles Trevelyan actually resigned from the government and founded the Union of Democratic Control to co-ordinate the activities of Liberal and Labour opponents of government policy. Francis, however, was closely involved with developments as Grey's deputy at the Foreign Office.

Cornubian, 13/08/14

FRANCIS ACLAND TO THE EDITOR OF 'THE CORNUBIAN'

Foreign Office, London, 11 August 1914

Dear Sir,

In my letter last week I expressed the hope that I might be able to write fully this week as to the events which led up to the war. But at this office many of us have worked seven twenty-four hour shifts this last week in settling the hundreds of questions which arise all the world over out of a great war, and though I have not done so well as that, I have been on duty from ten a.m. to twelve p.m. every day except one, and have therefore not had time to analyse and summarise the volume of correspondence respecting the European crisis which the Foreign Office has published.

But I should like to give my constituents some idea of what we have been thinking and feeling up here.

It has been a most curious time which has seemed twice as long as any other week in my life.

The impression which remains most vividly in my mind is that which I have received while I have been working at night. My room looks right across the Horse Guard's Parade to the great Admiralty building of which every window has been brightly lighted. And I have seen and listened to the cheering of the crowds moving up and down Whitehall on one side, and of the greater crowd outside Buckingham Palace across the park, on the other side, and the fierce bursts of singing and cheering outside the German Embassy opposite, near the Duke of York's column – while the great building was left dark and empty by the departure of the German Ambassador, who had worked so hard to preserve friendly relations. And all the time they moved slowly close past my window in the dark, great beams drawn up from below which have been built into a platform on the roof, from which the Admiralty wireless station is now being safeguarded against attacks by aircraft.

The crowds for the first few days were very great, and Downing Street had to be kept clear of them, and I could always see in the day time a great mass of men at the far end of it, in Whitehall, waiting for the Cabinet Ministers to pass to and from the Houses of Commons, and a crowd below my window at the other end of it watching the Ambassadors visiting the Foreign Office, and in Downing Street itself, almost empty, with only the officials hurrying across from the different departments to keep the Cabinet and the Prime Minister informed of all the latest telegraphic information.

I was a Civil Servant at the time of the Boer War. There is a great contrast between that time and this. There is very little "Mafeking" this time.[1] The streets have been full of Regulars and Territorials, but I have not seen one the worse for drink. There are a few street hawkers in Whitehall selling mourning cards for Germany. That is foolishness, for the great struggle is only at its beginning, and I think the crowds know it, and the men do little trade. In general, I think we feel a vague awe and amazement at the prospect of the clash of the millions of men and the great battleships. There will be misery and destruction and change on a scale of which we have no experience, and in ways which we cannot foresee. We feel the vague discomfort of a man who has to undergo an operation, and though there is splendid courage and confidence the discomfort remains.

The great change, however, in the last fifteen years is the improvement in the working of the public services. We are infinitely better prepared for an emergency than we were. At the War Office and the Admiralty the machine is working splendidly and silently. No one knows where the men or the ships are, but we should know fast enough if they were in their wrong places. There is the inevitable rush of persons with all sorts of ideas wishing to improvise schemes, but the military, social and industrial organisation of the nation is now so good that the right action in general cases is to expand the machinery that exists rather than to improvise new. "Business carried on as usual" is our motto here, just as it should be, and no doubt is, the motto of your readers in Cornwall.

And what can I say of the great causes which have drawn this Empire into war. A few points stand out, besides that which Mr. Asquith has explained so clearly.

1. Germany could have prevented a war between Austria and Russia. Russia did not want to prevent Austria from obtaining satisfaction from Serbia, but while Austria refused to set a reasonable limit to that satisfaction, Russia felt bound to begin preparations which would have enabled her to intervene. Germany could have induced Austria to fix such reasonable limits, but she did not do so.

2. IF THERE WAS BOUND TO BE WAR between Germany and France and Russia, Germany was in great danger, unless she could crush France before Russia was fully prepared to strike. So much we must admit. But did this justify Germany in striking so suddenly and wantonly at France? The answer is "No". It cannot be shown that Russia or France contemplated an aggressive attack on Germany. It can be shown that had this been their intention, or that of either of them, all our influence, and it would have been great, must have been used to hold them back.

3. If then Germany could have prevented Russian action against Austria, if she could have relied on Russia and France refraining from attack on herself, her attack upon France was military tyranny – the act of a soldier despot, not of a civilised State. It is the business of the people of Europe to see that such acts can never be committed again.

4. What about Belgium? Germany and England undertook to preserve Belgium from attack in return for imposing upon her the obligation of not attacking anyone else. Germany has broken her word, England has kept hers. The principle of sanctity of treaty rights is really the test of the progress of civilization, as compared to a state of force and lawlessness. It is the foundation of all confidence between nations. We had to break our word or keep it – there was no middle course, for nothing would have kept Germany back from violating Belgian neutrality. I am glad we kept our word. It makes for war now, but it will make for peace ultimately. But there is something more to be said. When the great Powers guaranteed the neutrality of Belgium, they did more than simply undertake a solemn engagement. Belgium's security under the

treaty meant to a large extent the security of Western Europe from war. A neutral country between two great Powers is like a large pillow put down between two small children. It makes their quarrelling more difficult, and as long as neither strikes at the other across it there may be peace in the nursery. Our interest is peace – so we must prevent countries striking at one another across neutralised states.

This is all I have time to write. It will be a hideous, long, grim struggle – not a matter of weeks but of months, perhaps of years. It will need all our courage and resolution and endurance to push it through. This we must all give – but our great object must be not only to win – but to make it impossible that such a struggle should ever again be waged upon the earth.

Yours faithfully,

F.D. Acland

[1.] News of the famous relief of the South African town of Mafeking in May 1900 led to wild and intemperate scenes of celebration in London. The event had provided a psychological boost to the British population during the Boer war.

DRO, 1148 M/616

FRANCIS ACLAND TO ELEANOR ACLAND

20 August 1914

Dearest,

I'm back from work about 7 after a hardish day. Things are not going too well, but as well as to be expected. The Belgians when it came to fighting regular battles did not apparently make much of a stand.[1] Our people are at Maubeuge where it was always arranged they should be, & the Germans are supposed to be pushing straight at them & the French there, or trying to get round both us & the French between Maubeuge & Lille which will be a dangerous manoeuvre for them. The only thing that matters so far as we are concerned is that our people are where they were meant to be when they were meant to be, and will be almost for certain at a very lot earlier indeed in the first really big battle. I wish I were there rather.

Grey in telling me about this told me also that Asquith had been strongly opposed to my transfer to the War Office. So that's that.

. . . I have been practically dictating the telegrams they are to send to the different capitals [about arrangements for the return of British citizens] & I hope they are sent off by now. I expect the big battle will be about Saturday & Sunday & if the Germans can't break through the general belief is that they are done.

1. Refers to the ease with which Germans forces had been able to force the Belgian army back to Antwerp and occupy Brussels by 20 August.

DRO, 1148 M/617

FRANCIS ACLAND TO ELEANOR ACLAND

21 August 1914

Dearest,

I write today just before going back. Father & I lunched with Grey & Haldane[1] – most amicable & pleasant, & father met Runciman [2] outside afterwards & walked off with him. I showed Haldane Spender's [3] letter & my part of the "w[estminster]. g[azette]" about the Army. He thinks Asquith is particularly anxious to avoid making [illegible] & in a vague way is sure K[itchener].[4] is doing & will do fine work – but more I thought in order to persuade himself that he had been right in putting K[itchener]. there than with real conviction.

We hear that the Germans have demanded [money?] from Brussels & that they are today at Ghent & expected at Ostend tomorrow. I pity them if they get within reach of our ships.

Our military people are quite confident as to the situation. They think the Germans are risking all & that it may very likely become a Sedan[5] for them.

Grey said he had saved £3000 to spend in six years on salmon fishing after the Gov[ermen]t. went out & that he is giving it all to relief funds. Turkey[6] is having a high old time trying to make terms both with Germany & us as if she had conquered us both. We are being polite but not losing our heads.

1. Richard Burdon Haldane (1856–1928) was first elected as a Liberal MP in 1885 and became Minister for War in 1905. Elevated to the peerage in 1911, he became Lord Chancellor in the following year and remained in this post until press hostility led to his dismissal in 1915. He returned to office as Lord Chancellor in the Labour administration of 1924.

2. Walter Runciman (1870–1949) was first elected as a Liberal MP in 1899 and became President of the Board of Trade in 1914. He resigned in 1916 with Asquith but was again President of the Board of Trade 1931–37 as a Liberal National member of the National Government. Represented the Cornish seat of St Ives 1929–37. Created Viscount Runciman in 1937.

3. John Alfred Spender (1862–1942) was the editor of the pro-Liberal *Westminster Gazette* 1896–1921. After resigning from the paper because of his association with the Asquithian cause he wrote a number of major biographies. He was president of the traditionalist Liberal Council 1936–42.

4. Horatio Herbert Kitchener (1850–1916) was appointed Secretary of State at the War Office at the outbreak of war. This move was intended to encourage public confidence in the war effort due to Kitchener's reputation as a war hero in Sudan and South Africa. He was created Earl Kitchener of Khartoum in 1914 but drowned two years later when his ship was sunk on the way to Russia.

5. Refers to the historic defeat of the French forces at the Battle of Sedan in September 1870. This critical event in the Franco-Prussian war 1870–71 after just seven weeks of fighting led to the fall of France's Second Empire.

6. In the event Turkey decided in October 1914 to enter the war on the side of Germany and the Austro-Hungarian Empire.

DRO, 1148 M/618

FRANCIS ACLAND TO ELEANOR ACLAND

September 1914?

I am taking on a good deal more work, but it will be interesting – & I think the only way not to be v[ery]. miserable about the war is to work at something quite hard.

DRO, 1148 M/619

FRANCIS ACLAND TO ELEANOR ACLAND

Autumn 1914?

I'm on the front bench – waiting for the adjournment on which I have to speak. I've just seen C. V. Thomas[1] who is sitting up in the Gallery – & very pleased with the meeting he had at Camborne. Vivian[2] also writes that he was pleased & that he did splendidly but C.V. says Vivian almost spoilt the meeting. I'm having a boring time as I can't get Licock [?] or anyone else to get . . . on with the work that Masterman[3] wants from his authors. I say "get out a short statement about bomb dropping on undefended towns" and they come back 3 hours later to say that they can't do anything [illegible] two days and a legal advisor. It makes me long to . . . do it all myself, but I know that that would not be right really. I shall get them working soon but they are by training so desperately afraid of committing themselves about anything, and the literary gents want material red hot.

[1] Charles V. Thomas (1860–1941) was the head of a prominent Wesleyan and mining family in West Cornwall and a leading member of the Camborne Liberal Association.

[2] Probably John Vivian who was a member of Cornwall County Council and another prominent local Liberal.

[3] Charles Frederick Gurney Masterman (1873–1927) was head of the War Propaganda Bureau. He was responsible for recruiting writers, artists and photographers to help with the war effort. Before the war he had been a government minister at the Home Office 1909–12 and the Treasury 1912–14. He was Liberal MP for West Ham North 1906–14 and Rusholme 1923–24.

DRO, 1148 M/620

FRANCIS ACLAND TO ELEANOR ACLAND

Autumn 1914

It was mostly a meeting under Masterman with the leading press men of the country about how to make a good showing in neutral countries in which for about 2 hours I had to hold the fort & did fairly well. I'm to have an extra private secretary & to be in charge of all the arrangements, but its interesting &, I think it may be, useful work so I'm glad to take it on.

DRO, 1148 M/26

HERBERT ASQUITH TO FRANCIS ACLAND

10, Downing Street, London, 28 May 1915

My dear Acland,

Thank you for your letter. In the circumstances, I shall be grateful if you will represent the Board of Agriculture in the House of Commons. I am asking the King to make you a Privy Councillor.

Yours sincerely,

H.H. Asquith

DRO, 1148 M/624

FRANCIS ACLAND TO ELEANOR ACLAND

24 August 1915

I've been dictating a long letter to Selborne[1] about his coming speech to the farmers' bodies on Thursday. I'm afraid he'll make a great parade all about nothing & that it'll come to this – The State won't do anything for you but it's your patriotic duty to do it for yourselves. This is true but won't be well received. He's going to have County Committees set up, but has no idea what powers or duties they will have, & I feel people will just say – more machinery. I've tried to suggest real work for the Committees, but whether the [illegible] a wee bit too stupid to modify what he's going to say now is more than I know.

Carkeek looked in this morning. He says my speech produced a wonderful effect. I apparently talked to a powerful lot of Tories, and they all come to him and say "Our member – what a <u>beautiful</u> man".

---

[1] William Palmer (1859–1942) was President of the Board of Agriculture 1915–16. He succeeded to the title of Earl of Selborne in 1895 and it was left to Acland as Parliamentary Secretary to speak on agriculture in the Commons. Selborne was a Conservative peer and First Lord of the Admiralty 1900–05.

DRO, 1148 M/625

FRANCIS ACLAND TO ELEANOR ACLAND

26 August 1915

Selborne made a really good speech today – a fine mixture of eloquence & commonsense, & great loyalty to the Gov[ernmen]t. I'll send you a full report if I can. Bathurst[1] speaking for the farmers had sense enough to back him up & say that farmers will do their best if the Gov[ermen]t gave them anything or nothing. So all went very well.

1. Presumably Sir Charles Bathurst (1867–1958) who was a Conservative MP and regarded as a leading expert on agriculture. He was Parliamentary Secretary at the Ministry of Food Control 1916–17 and Parliamentary Secretary at the Ministry of Agriculture & Fisheries 1924–28. Became Baron Bledisloe in 1918 and a Viscount in 1935.

DRO, 1148 M/629

FRANCIS ACLAND TO ELEANOR ACLAND

1 September 1915

CH[1] told me last night that Sir Ian Hamilton[2] did not expect ever to get through at the Dardanelles. There was a time when they started the new landings on the N[orth]. side of the peninsula when if he'd had a good general he could have done it but Hunter Weston[3] who was splendid has been invalided home. An old fellow called Stopford[4] had been sent out (as the best they could do) who just lacked the push required to order a big general advance when they began to be held up. French[5] wont let Ian H[amilton]. have any good man from France, & wont do anything himself. I am getting to the stage of not being able to see how on earth we can win.

1. Possibly Sir Charles Harris (1864–1943) who joined the Civil Service in 1886 and became Joint Secretary of the War Office 1920–24.
2. Sir Ian Hamilton (1853–1947) was commander of the allied expeditionary forces in the Dardanelles. This expedition was envisaged as a way of forcing Turkey out of the war but it was a military disaster for the allied cause. Hamilton was criticised for his negative attitude on the likelihood of a successful evacuation and was dismissed from command on 15 October 1915.

3. Sir Aylmer Gould Hunter-Weston (1864–1940) was in command of the British 29th Division that landed at Cape Helles near the Dardanelles in March 1915. Nicknamed 'The Butcher of Helles', he was invalided from Gallipoli in July but played a controversial role in the Sommes campaign in 1916. He was Conservative MP for North Ayrshire (later Bute and Northern) 1916–35.

4. Sir Frederick William Stopford (1854–1929) was surprisingly transferred from the ceremonial post of Lieutenant of the Tower of London to lead the allied attack in Gallipoli. He was criticised for a disastrous offensive at Sulva Bay and sent back to Britain in August 1915.

5. Sir John Denton Pinkstone French (1852–1925) commanded the British Expeditionary Force in France. Growing criticism of his style of leadership led to his replacement by Douglas Haig in December 1915. He then served as Commander of the British Home Forces 1915–18 and became Earl of Ypres.

DRO, 1148 M/638

FRANCIS ACLAND TO ELEANOR ACLAND

16 August 1916

I think I'm going to write to Grey asking him to see Asquith if there's any chance of a new man going to the Ed[ucatio]n Office. They ought to take me if there's anything besides a shuffle but they won't.[1]

1. In the event the Marquis of Crewe, a Liberal peer, was appointed as the President of the Board of Education on 18 August 1916. He replaced Arthur Henderson, the Labour leader, who became Paymaster General.

West Briton, 11/12/16

FRANCIS ACLAND TO CAMBORNE LIBERAL ASSOCIATION

5 December 1916

These are very difficult times, in which any member of Parliament needs all the patience and trust and support that his constituents can give him. I do not at all like what I hear about the possible reorganisation of affairs it seems to me that we want steady men just now, not nervous and excitable ones, but I suppose the best thing that any of us can do is just to stick to the job that we can do best as long as we are privileged to be able to do good work in it, and for the rest to have faith and patience. It is a dark time, but I hope it is a case of the darkest hour before the dawn.

1. Refers to the events leading up to the fall of the Asquith administration. Asquith resigned as Prime Minister on 5 December and Lloyd George was invited to form a new government on the following day.

West Briton, 21/12/16

FRANCIS ACLAND TO SIR ARTHUR CARKEEK

19 December 1916

My dear Carkeek,

As you will, I think, have expected, I have been carrying on with my ordinary work through the political crisis. But as I see in this morning's papers, the name of my successor[1] at the Board of Agriculture and Fisheries, I have not unnaturally concluded that I need not carry on any longer. This decision of the Prime Minister, as you know, accords exactly with my hopes and determination, and I have now a justification and indeed a duty, to lay aside other work that I happened to be doing besides Parliamentary Secretary to the Board.

I am therefore asking leave to resign my Chairmanship of the Forage Committee, the Timber Supplies Committee, the Pit-timber Committee, the Fertilizers Committee, the sub-committee of the Cabinet Reconstruction Committee on Afforestation, the Indian Wheat Committee (which has practically finished its work) and the Potato Committee (which has recently started and framed the order as to seed-potatoes which was published this morning).

You and my other friends may be interested in knowing what I think I ought now to do. When I was certain that I could not remain in office, I naturally applied for a transfer from the London University Officers' Training Corps to a battalion from which I should be sure to go on active service in due course. I thought I could obtain such a transfer, but I find that my doctor is practically certain that if I went on service I should be invalided out in a very short time.[2]

This seems to make it my duty to abandon the idea, though it is a real disappointment to me. If I can obtain fairly soon any full-time work which would clearly be of more value to the State than my trying to fight I am therefore willing to do anything I can to help the new President of the Board of Agriculture[3] or anyone else who thinks my work would be of use.

I will report to you, and through you to my constituents, how things go as soon as I can, and meanwhile I hope to get a chance of coming down to see them.

There is no doubt, I think, that their duty is just the same as yours and mine: namely, to support the new Government to the utmost of our power for the duration of the war, and to serve it in any possible way we can.

Yours most truly,

F.D. Acland

[1] His successor on 14 December 1916 was Sir Richard Winfrey (1858–1944). Winfrey served as Secretary to the Board of Agriculture and Fisheries 1916–19 and was Liberal (then Lloyd George Liberal) MP for South West Norfolk until 1923. He was Liberal MP for Gainsborough 1923–24.

[2] Acland suffered from severe asthma and related health problems for much of his life.

[3] Roland Edmund Prothero (1851–1937) was a writer and President of the Board of Agriculture and Fisheries 1916–19. He had been Conservative MP for Oxford University and was later created Lord Ernle. Prothero was a leading exponent of a more pro-active food production policy.

DRO, 1148 M/648

FRANCIS ACLAND TO ELEANOR ACLAND

31 January 1917

Yes the Speaker's Conference[1] resolutions mean progress. We get a lot of things we've wanted for some time and I think things are so that if anything is done at all women must get votes unless we suffs play the utter ass. Its difficult to know what to do about suffrage. I think the plan proposed beginning at 35 would be too narrow to start with, but if it began at 30 I should be content to start with it rather than risk the whole thing by making it possible for [illegible] to say that we couldn't agree on the form. One of the difficulties of rushing about all at once is that the Labour people, though most effusive in lip service don't *really* want the ordinary unmarried woman worker to have a vote, at least until they've settled labour things on their own lines.

There's no Whitaker[2] [?] in this house so I can't tell if Camborne would go. I think it's just well over the 50,000 which I regret for if it were abolished or merged I should be free. But there will be such a fine old jumble up that one will be able to claim some freedom without unfairness to Camborne. Goodness knows whether the House will be sensible enough to let a bill be drafted & go through, or whether they'll piffle at small points & make it necessary for the bill to be withdrawn.[3]

[1.] The Speaker's Conference on Electoral Reform met between October 1916 and January 1917. It was established with all-party approval by the Speaker of the House of Commons, to consider four major issues: the introduction of female suffrage; an extension of male suffrage; the introduction of proportional representation and the redistribution of parliamentary constituencies. The Speaker's Conference paved the way for the Representation of the People Act 1918.

[2.] A reference to the famous *Whitaker's Almanack* founded by Joseph Whitaker in 1868. It includes factual and statistical information relating to British politics.

[3.] Francis's pro-active support for female suffrage and proportional representation provides another reason for his refusal to oppose the proposed reduction in Cornwall's parliamentary representation (see below). Since these measures were connected he was more concerned with the implementation of a wider reform package rather than local redistribution issues.

DRO, 1148 M/651

FRANCIS ACLAND TO ELEANOR ACLAND

3 February 1917

I hope America is soon [?] in.[1] I still think the war will be over by midsummer. I think Germany wants to be able to show its jingoes that it's tried everything & then be able to say that it must give in against the whole world in arms. The German ships in USA will come in very handy. I think it's the best thing that's happened since the war began. Our people don't realise how difficult it was to go on getting American currency & steel & whatever America does or doesn't do in other ways, were certain to get them all right as long as we want them – if we can get them over.

[1.] The United States of America declared war on 4 April 1917. Pressure had been steadily mounting following Germany's declaration in January that it regarded all ships trading with Britain as legitimate targets. The loss of American merchant vessels was compounded by revelations that Germany intended to support Mexico in a border war with the USA.

Bodleian Library, Asquith papers, MS. Asquith 18, fols 1–5

FRANCIS ACLAND TO HERBERT ASQUITH

93 Bedford Gardens, London, 18 February 1917

My dear Chief,

Ll[oyd] G[eorge]'s speech is to deal with land questions so you may perhaps find it useful to have some notes from me on the points which he may refer to. I am doing whole time work for Prothero – in many ways much the same work as I did before (Winfrey not counting) – but I have been careful not to ask Prothero or others which was likely to be done, so I can write freely, though I can only guess at the line that may be taken.

1. Prothero tentatively suggested to some of his advisors a fortnight ago a scheme offering a bonus to farmers for every acre put under seed from this date onward – in order to make up for the low prices fixed, or likely to be fixed by Devonport.[1] I thought it a suggestion open to much criticism. First because it proceeds on the assumption that the farmer is an unpatriotic shirker who can only be stimulated to full efforts by the prospect of reward – whereas to do the farmer justice – he is in the vast majority of cases doing all he possibly can with the labour at his disposal. But my chief criticism was that the method was so clearly a subterfuge to get around Devonport. The Gov[ernmen]t either does or does not wish the consumer to get produce at less than cost of production plus a fair profit. If it does not, Devonport's prices should be fair and should need no extra bonus. If it does it would be far better to commandeer at a fair price, and sell to the public at less – explaining and justifying the payment of the difference by the taxpayer – than to make up the difference between a fair and an unfair price in the guise of a bonus on production.

   Others made similar criticisms of the idea and it may well be that it will not have survived.

2. It is more probable that Ll[oyd]. G[eorge] will outline a future policy for agriculture.[2] This policy will probably be on the lines of the interim report which the Agricultural Policy sub-committee of the (late) Cabinet Reconstruction Committee under Lord Selborne is just about to bring out. Milner[3] is I know very keen on it, and may well have got Ll[oyd]. G[eorge] to adopt it. It will base agric[ultural]. reconstruction on three planks:- guaranteed minimum prices for wheat (42/–) and oats (21/–), a guaranteed minimum wage for agric[ultural]. labour (not fixed) and maximum production from the soil

   (with regard to the first you make like a figure. If wheat prices become again what they were during the average of seven years before the war (33/–) and we grew half the wheat we consume (17 million quarters) instead of 1/5 (seven million quarters) a 42/– guarantee would cost the taxpayer about 7½ million pounds a year. Of oats we already grow 20 million quarters out of 27 consumed. If we grew all we need I think we might have to pay 5 million pounds, but my figures are not so exact as for wheat)

I believe that a policy of this kind will be very simply pressed but it is not a thing to be rushed or adopted in a hurry. The point about it as to which I feel very strongly is that its general acceptance by the country should depend upon the extent to which the requirement of maximum production is enforced as the centre of the policy. If maximum production is seriously enforced there is no doubt that farmers must have a reasonable chance of making it pay and the means that they must be protected from such a slump in wheat prices as occurred about the end of last century. With this guarantee to them the guarantee to the labourer of decent conditions and pay goes by common consent. But if the enforcement of full utilisation of land, instead of being the pivot of the whole policy, is merely eye wash – of many powerful influences would like it to be – the farmers and landowners will get a steady dole of taxpayers money for an entirely inadequate return. Decent agric[ultural] wages and conditions for labour were bound to come anyhow, – on no other conditions after the war can labour be got back onto the land, and the farmer in no way deserves that as a set off against having to pay a decent wage he should get permanent protection for his main crops. Imagine the town citizen's view:- "Are we to pay those blighters 12 millions a year because for the first time in their lives they have got to do what we've made every foreign sweating Jewish tailor do long ago, – pay decent wages".

From this point of view I think it very important to insist on enforced maximum soil utilisation as the centre of any new policy from the very first. If we saw from year to year that a steadily increasing proportion of our food supply was being produced here, and if, following upon searching surveys, bad landlords and tenants were having their land taken away from them without compensation the policy would stand criticism, and be I think for the general good. But it would do very little good and would not stand criticism if increased production only meant spending more money on agric[ultural]. research & education and demonstration by the State of what could be done – farmers & landowners being left to do very much as they liked.

3. Ll[oyd]. G[eorge] will I think talk of timber. A new plan is being brought out, and, as a plan, it is good. Hitherto there has been no control of timber production at home or abroad (where the waste of timber has

been prodigious) and timber production at home has been run by the Home Grown Timber Committee which appointed by the Board of Agriculture – has had little authority for getting men and plant except that which I have been able to exert as its Chairman. Now they are going to put the whole of production and consumption at home and abroad under one man – Sir Bampfylde Fuller[4] – and, being unwilling to set up yet another new Ministry, he is to be, nominally, a Director under the War Office. My committee therefore which has really done good work, is to be disbanded, though I remain as the representative of the Board of Agriculture on a committee which will advise Fuller – if he chooses to consult it. If Fuller succeeds in stimulating production in France, which has hitherto been held back because the French will not let us fell their woods, – and in checking the waste there, and in getting more labour and plant than we have managed to get – he will do well and much tonnage can be saved. But when I saw him I thought him a doctrinaire ex-Indian Governor of the worst sort, and far too old for the job, and, I am not hopeful. Everything as to production here depends upon whether he can prevent Geddes,[5] the director of recruiting, from capturing for the Army the men without whose labour his brother the younger Geddes[6] makes of roads & railways in France cannot get the timber to make them:- and from this point of view it is well to have made Fuller a co-director of the War Office with Geddes the elder . . .

4. It may be well to point out that no bonus on future sowing of crops, no sketch of the future agricultural policy of the country, no rearrangement of timber organisation, will really supply the lack of skill of labour which is the fundamental difficulty at present. These men are in many cases acting as officers, servants and grooms, and are kept tight hold of by French in the Home Defence Army and I have seen no definite sign hitherto of an effective count-out. The War Office promises continually but their promises come to nothing.

Excuse this great length. I only write as you know so as to be of some possible service.

Yours sincerely, F.D. Acland

[1.] Sir Hudson Kearley (1856–1934) was Food Controller 1916–17. He was Liberal MP for Plymouth Devonport 1892–1910 and Parliamentary Secretary at the Board of Trade 1905–9. Kearley was created Baron Devonport in 1910 and became a Viscount in 1917.

[2.] Refers to the discussions leading up to the introduction of the Corn Production Bill, which was passed in August 1917. The bill covered guaranteed prices in 1917 of 60s for wheat and 38s for oats, a minimum wage of 25s a week, rent restriction and the control of cultivation. P.E. Dewey, *British Agriculture in the First World War,* London, 1989, points out that Liberal and Labour members were critical of the idea of guaranteed prices on the grounds that it was 'enriching one section of the community at the expense of the rest' (p. 93). This attitude is reflected in Francis's letter to Asquith and also in his comments in DRO, 1148 M/661.

3. Sir Alfred Milner (1854–1925) became Viscount Milner in 1902 and High Commissioner for South Africa 1897–1905. He was a Conservative member of the War Cabinet 1916–18, Secretary of State for War 1918–19 and Secretary of State for the Colonies 1919–21.

4. Sir Joseph Bamfylde Fuller (1854–1935) was an author and a pre-war administrator in India. He was appointed secretary of revenue and agriculture in India in 1901 and became Lieutenant Governor of Eastern Bengal and Assam in 1905. During the First World War he initially served as a major in the Army Ordinance Corps before becoming director of timber supplies at the War Office in 1917.

5. Sir Auckland Campbell Geddes (1879–1954) was Conservative MP for Basingstoke 1917–20 and became Lord Geddes in 1942. He was Director of Recruiting 1916–17, Minister of National Service 1917–19, President of the Board of Local Government 1918–19, Minister for Reconstruction 1919 and President of the Board of Trade 1919–20.

6. Sir Eric Campbell Geddes (1875–1937) was Conservative MP for Cambridge 1917–22. He served in the Lloyd George Coalition government as First Lord of the Admiralty 1917–19, Minister without Portfolio 1919 and Minister of Transport 1919–21. Francis describes him as 'the younger Geddes' but he was actually four years older than his brother.

DRO, 1148 M/655

FRANCIS ACLAND TO ELEANOR ACLAND

February 1917

Asquith's a pig. I sent him on Monday a full & really helpful letter about land, & he hasn't sent me a line of thanks.

DRO, 1148 M/654

FRANCIS ACLAND TO ELEANOR ACLAND

23 March 1917

The news today is that the agriculture bill will come in on Tuesday and I shall speak I think. And Spender will take an article from me to appear in his Tuesday's number – but limits it to 1500 words. As my stuff was about 5000 I have had a deuce of a job but the little lady has taken it down & is typing & combing now & I hope it wont be much over the 1500. I shall have tomorrow to cut & [?] so I ought to get it pretty decent. On Sunday I can get it into speech form. Its so long since I've made a speech in the House that was any good that I don't half look forward to it.

———————

DRO, 1148 M/656

FRANCIS ACLAND TO ELEANOR ACLAND

Spring 1917

There is to be a general discussion on the Corn Production Bill tomorrow in the House which ought to give me a good chance. I think the ex-ministers are to be allowed to go as they please so I shall be free to expatiate, and I shall be a fool unless I can make a good fist of it. I must try this evening to get things fixed up so that I can get in a good place.

———————

DRO, 1148 M/661

FRANCIS ACLAND TO ELEANOR ACLAND

1917

I've heard Ll[oyd]. G[eorge] and on the whole I'm glad the big agriculture [?] job is started. But he might have put it so much better. Runciman at my prompting did. I hate having to face paying say £15 million to farmers just as a quid pro quo for their paying decent wages. Runciman brought out the fact that 25/– is less than 16/– was in real wages which was useful.

———————

DRO, 1148 M/665

FRANCIS ACLAND TO ELEANOR ACLAND

25 May 1917

I've just got a nice letter from Middleton[1] which I send you to look at. I really think I was quite right to go, though no doubt I could have suggested to Lee[2] ways of rearranging the work which would both have made things possible for Middleton and have provided useful work for me. I couldn't quite bring myself to scramble to keep in there, if the head of the place had made a plan which meant my going, and hadn't dreamt of trying to see whether he couldn't do what he wanted and yet keep me. I didn't see many of the members of the Committee before I went, but those I did see made it quite clear that I had been a real help. They said [?] had chiefly been in making them keep a broad general point of view in mind in writing and producing their technical stuff, and also in fighting their battles with outsiders. They felt too that I was a real friend of science & education – & liked me – and I them. Its quite likely that the turn of the wheel will bring us together again, and I hope it will.

Now that I'm well & freer I ought to get some meetings in Camborne polished off before hay time comes along. So I've proposed to Heath[3] to have meetings next Friday & Saturday & perhaps the Monday too – coming back for Parliament starting again on the Tuesday.

---

[1] Sir T.H. Middleton was senior civil servant at the Board of Agriculture and Fisheries and briefly Director General of the Food Production Department (FPD) in January–February 1917.

[2] Sir Arthur Lee (1868–1947) had been appointed as Director General of the FPD in February 1917. His abrasive style was intended to make the organisation an effective body (see Dewey, *British Agriculture in the First World War*, p. 97). Lee was a Conservative MP and Minister of Agriculture and Fisheries 1919–21. He became Baron Lee in 1918 and a Viscount in 1922.

[3] George Heath was the Liberal party's agent for the Camborne constituency. He later became Isaac Foot's agent in Bodmin.

DRO, 1148 M/666

FRANCIS ACLAND TO ELEANOR ACLAND

26 May 1917

I shall have lots to do in making the speeches I shall have to fire off in Cornwall. I must try to understand & make them understand what the Russian Revol[utio]n[1] means for now & the future and what Liberalism has still got to do.

I believe that all the bullying of soldiers & doctors & tribunals & the proving [?] of these new business ministers will "come to good" eventually and produce a very healthy reaction. It will be a fine thing that wealth will be much more difficult and work much more necessary. A union of great democracies – including Germany – against war & aggression seems to me much more possible now than ever before after the war. And it seems to me less probable than it did that we shall let ourselves be bossed & exploited by capitalists.

[1.] The first Russian revolution had resulted in the abdication of Tsar Nicholas II in March 1917. A Provisional Government was formed with the intention of convening a constituent assembly and the allies welcomed its decision to continue the war effort.

DRO, 1148 M/667

FRANCIS ACLAND TO ELEANOR ACLAND

28 May 1917

I've got the Cornish meetings fixed up, three of them Fri[day], Sat[urday], Monday. I get back on Tuesday afternoon for the night trains been taken off. It's a bore to spend five days over three meetings, but can't be helped. Cornwall will under redistribution boil down from seven to four seats – possibly five. I think I must be free to go elsewhere for Camborne is I think going Labour as fast as it can, and no other Cornish seat is very desirable. The new election will be a queer time when it comes!

DRO, 1148 M/668

FRANCIS ACLAND TO ELEANOR ACLAND

31 May 1917

I can't get into words what I really feel about Russia. It's too big. However, I'll try to make the good citizens of St Day Lanner & St Agnes think a bit, but probably all they'll be keen about is that the Gov[ernmen]t should not tackle the Drink question, in order to avoid being defeated.

DRO, 1148 M/669

FRANCIS ACLAND TO ELEANOR ACLAND

Sunday 3 June 1917

They are a rum lot down here, St Agnes, where the old boy talked to you about the sinfulness of feeling happy or something of that sort, is going to be cut off from the Mining Division. But I met the Liberals there last night and gave them as good a talk as I could and told them repeatedly how sorry I should be to lose them. There was a good deal of discussion whether it would be better for them to go or stay, but not a soul of the lot of them had the grace to say that if they were cut off they'd be sorry to lose me as their member. And so it is throughout. They grumble furiously if I don't come & aren't in the least pleased or interested if I do.

The reshuffle which has just been proposed by the boundary commissioners is interesting. Cornwall's seven members are reduced to five & we have attached to us Penryn Falmouth, a corrupt & rotten borough, the rural parishes of the present Truro Helston division that lie in between our division & Falmouth & the whole thing is to be called the P.F (Penryn Falmouth) division though they contribute less than 1/7 of the population.[1] There will be two sitting members Goldman[2] & I & we shall I suppose oppose one another if we both want to go on. It will be a good chance for me to make my own terms or move elsewhere. Falmouth has been accustomed to have men like Horniman[3] or John Barker[4] of Kensington as its Liberal candidates & I feel inclined to say that I shall not stand unless (1) invited unanimously with pledges of real support by the Liberals of Falmouth & the new parts of Truro division as well as here & (2) unless they will together be quite content with the subscription which I give at present. I think that very likely they will say 'no' which would give me a decent excuse for getting out & going elsewhere. There ought to be some pretty safe Liberal seats newly created that will want to get good men so there should be a good chance. On paper the new division here should be pretty safe for the new parts of Truro that come will be more Liberal than Tory & Falmouth is pretty even when heavily bought by the Liberals, and has only about a 300 Tory majority when it isn't. What effect a labour man would have I don't at all know – but with the transferable vote I ought to push through even then.

It seems to me to be rather silly to write like this, as the Lord [?] only knows how things are going to work out and whether there's going to be a Tory and a Liberal party any more. The right line seems to be to sit pretty loose to things here for a bit till one finds out a little more how things are likely to go but to get the Liberals in the new constituency together as soon as possible & induce them to show their hand as to what they want. There are rumours of a labour man, F.C. Eddy[5], the present treasurer of our association! He has definitely suggested it to several, but I'm sure its only a move on his part to get put on the bench, on the "if you don't put me on the bench at once I'll become labour candidate" stunt! As he's only 35 it shows a good bit of swelled head I think! – and I don't think the [illegible] will work. If it doesn't and he stands it would do us very little harm, for he's not a working man, has no reputation and very little influence.

I had a good time yesterday. A Tory neighbour of Carkeek's, retired stockbroker, was going to motor him over to Newquay to play golf, but he's crocked with neuritis, so the man took me instead. It's a jolly time at this time of year . . . Lady C[arkeek] "her ladyship" is in bed with colitis so things are quiet here. I want to get a good walk up Carn Brea this afternoon but Carkeek wants to take me around a new estate he's bought so I shan't get a decent tramp. I wish you were here, so that we could curse the Cornish together.

1. This option was eventually rejected by the Boundary Commission. It was decided instead to combine the pre-war constituency of St Austell with the towns and rural hinterland of Penryn, Falmouth and Truro to form the new constituency of Penryn & Falmouth.
2. Charles Sydney Goldman (1868–1958) was Unionist MP for Penryn, Falmouth & Flushing January 1910–18.
3. Frederick John Horniman (1835–1906) was a wealthy tea merchant, a noted entomologist and the founder of the Horniman Museum in London. He was Liberal MP for Penryn, Falmouth & Flushing 1895–1906.
4. Sir John Barker (1840–1914) was founder of Barkers of Kensington, a popular London department store. He became an alderman of London County Council in 1889 and was briefly Liberal MP for Maidstone in 1900 before being unseated on petition. He was Liberal MP for Penryn, Falmouth & Flushing 1906–January 1910.

5. F.C. Eddy served as president of the Camborne Divisional Labour Party after the First World War.

—————————

Cornish Post, 21/06/17

FRANCIS ACLAND TO THE *CORNISH POST*

June 1917

During the parliamentary recess I was in the Mining Division, and took the opportunity of meeting my friends in St Day, St Agnes and Lanner. I think that some record of the impressions which I gained in our talks on public affairs may be of interest.

There was among those I met naturally much interest in the proposed change in the boundaries of the Parliamentary Divisions of Cornwall.[1] It is very hard lines if the county has to lose two members yet it seems clear that the Boundary Commissioners have gone even a little further than the strict letter of their instructions in giving five members. Rather more latitude has now been allowed to them owing to the decision of the House of Commons on June 11, but, though I listened very carefully to the statements made on behalf of the Government in the debate, I fear that nothing was said by the Home Secretary which indicated any likelihood of Cornwall getting any more members than it has been allotted.

I found in the Division the feeling that Liberals were honourably bound not to try to disturb the redistribution proposals of the general compromise, whatever they may think of them, as they are of course the result of the insistence by our political opponents on "one vote one value" whenever we have urged "One man one vote" and "One vote one value" inevitably means the loss of two Cornish seats. This is a pity, but it was felt we must not be less ready to accept that part of the compromise on which our political opponents lay particular stress than the rest of it, and that it would not be playing the game for us to try to upset the central principle.

There was also strong feeling that it was hard lines if the Mining Division, though incorporated almost whole into a new Division to which it would contribute two-thirds of the population, should be called by the name of a borough which, though most ancient and important, was not connected with our principal industry. It was, however, hoped that it might be possible, if boundaries are finally fixed as now proposed, to make some arrangements in the matter of name by common consent, as this would not be a matter in which any party interests were involved.

As to the war I found the general spirit as keen and steadfast as ever. At some previous meetings in the Division at the close of the year, I had ventured to predict that the war would not outlast the autumn. Since then the United States had entered the War and the Russian revolution had taken place, two of the most important events which had occurred in the history of the world, and both of these events had altered the prospects of peace. The entry of the United States put the ultimate issue beyond any doubt, and we must be most grateful and thankful that the Great Republic was now casting its full weight on the side of liberty.

And though Russia's inability to make her full weight felt at the present time seemed likely to delay a final result by making a decisive blow on the West more difficult, the new revolution was a splendid omen for the future of mankind, for it enormously increased the prospect of peace through a union of free democracies, each willing to respect the freedom of all. Such a peace seemed far more likely now that Russia had shown Germany the way to liberty and it seemed to us not unlikely that the present rulers of Germany, fearing a repetition there of what had happened in Russia, would not be willing or able to face another winter of war. But whether the war went on over the winter or not, it must continue until the policy expressed by the Russian Government, as interpreted by the democratic governments of France, the United States and Great Britain could be fully attained.

We discussed questions of food and drink. We were glad that the Ministry of Agriculture had declared that danger of starvation was over if only all of us would do what each of us can do to increase production and economise consumption of food. We resolved to do our very best to help. In spite of some differences of view on the temperance question, we hoped that the Government might be able to take advantage of the general spirit of unity in the nation to carry through by general consent some measure which would make the control and regulation of the drink traffic after the war, in accordance with the wishes of the people, more possible than it has hitherto been. We recognised that placing the Home Rule Act on the Statute Book[2] had led up to asking the people of Ireland to work out their own future for themselves, and wished the best possible success to the Convention which is about to assemble.

As to general affairs in this country, it was reported that irritation and unrest were being caused by the autocratic methods of some of those newly placed in authority, by the absence of a clear policy in food control, and by the lack of free discussion of labour questions; but it was recognised that for the present, feelings of this kind must be put aside so that everything might be done which could help towards a speedy victory.

F.D. ACLAND

[1.] The Speaker's Conference had recommended in January 1917 that the boundary commissioners for England & Wales should aim for an average population of about 70,000 per seat.

2. The outbreak of the First World War in August 1914 had led to the deferral of the implementation of the Government of Ireland Bill for the duration of the war.

———————

Cornish Post, 05/07/17

FRANCIS ACLAND TO EDITOR OF *WESTERN MORNING NEWS*

July 1917

Dear Sir,

My attention has been called to a paragraph quoted from "The Western Morning News" by "The Cornish Post" to which "The Post" puts the heading, "What does Mr Acland Fear in the Mining Division". It is pleasantly suggested in the paragraph, presumably because I said that Liberals were bound to respect the redistribution proposals which the present Reform Bill contains, that I shall be glad to have the Mining Division joined on to Penryn-Falmouth, as the Labour Party in the Mining Division want to turn me out, and if the division is enlarged it would "practically kill for ever the chance of a Labour member" sitting for the division.

This is all news to me, and I pass over the superior knowledge you have of the Labour party's intentions – and the solicitude which your party always shows for Labour – until it comes to a question of "deeds not words". I pass over your imputation that I must have a personal motive when dealing with public questions, for you are bound to judge men by your own stature, and presumably can do no other. But really you are very much mistaken if you think I want a larger division. A larger division means more expense and more work, and at a time when it seems to be my duty to stick tight to the civil and military work I am doing here this weighs heavily with me. Also, isn't it rather human to prefer to bear those good and ill-fortunes we have than fly to others that we know not of? And as for the chance of election, the one thing that seems to me certain is that at the next election and after we shall not know the old parties – Conservative, or Liberal, or Labour – any more as they have hitherto been known. I believe that there will be an entirely new division of parties, and can only look so far ahead as to suppose that with the transferable vote, a fairly practical social reformer, with a good deal of administrative experience, will stand a very good chance of being elected, however parties may divide, and however many candidates there may be. In fact the answer to your Note and "The Post's" question is that Mr. Acland fears nothing in the Mining Division, whether it remains as it is or is merged in a larger constituency.

But, sir, having dealt with your attempt at a personal score I come to the really important point, which is, "Can Cornwall claim six seats with any chance of success?" In common with everyone else connected with the county, I wish that she could, but if she cannot I would ask you to accept the position. After all, the redistribution proposals are put forward as part of a Government measure, and it is better, surely, at a time like this, not to be trying to raise up opposition to Government measures unless we have a very clear case. Let us see how the case stands. But, first of all, you prefer to misunderstand my reference to "one vote, one value". You pretend to think it means exactly equal divisions, and then you say that it could be carried out quite neatly by giving Cornwall six constituencies averaging 55,000. If there were to be exactly equal divisions Cornwall could only have four members, as I am sure you know quite well. But, as you also know, "one vote, one value" has been adopted as the Conservative counter proposal to "one man, one vote", as indicating the view that other electoral reforms must be accompanied by a redistribution of seats so as, in general broad principle, to give greater representation to those areas which have grown enormously since the last redistribution, and consequently fewer members to those areas which have not grown so much. (For we all, I think, agree that the membership of the House of Commons is not to be materially increased.)

Now this proposal on which, my political opponents (including yourself, if I am not much mistaken) have in the past laid great stress may simply be thrown to the winds. But if it is not – and I for one, consider myself honourably bound to try to get it fairly carried out – then, as I say, the question simply is whether it can be carried out with general fairness while keeping six seats for Cornwall. The proposal upon which the bill is based is that constituencies – averaging, as they must, about 75,000 population – should vary from a minimum of 50,000, to a maximum for a single member seat, of 120,000. A definite system of working this out is proposed, and under it five Cornish constituencies will average 66,000, which is well under the average for the whole country. If the Cornish average be reduced to 55,000 for six members, either there must be an entirely separate sort of treatment for town and country, and the big centres must lose several of the members they now expect to get, or the maximum of 120,000 for a single member seat must be much increased. I see no other ways – do you? – for I am sure you do not really believe that this can be dealt with solely as a Cornish question.[1]

Very well, then, is there any reasonable chance of getting the government or the country to accept either of these proposals? If so, let us try to work out a new system as an alternative to that in the bill. It is true that the

Government have at present refused to consider anything of the sort, with the exception of the small change in the instructions to the Boundary Commissioners which was recently made. But we might succeed where others have failed, and if anything of the sort looks at all promising, I would be very willing to help you and others to work it out and press it on the Government on the report stage of the bill.

But do not let us just go on saying, "Cornwall claims six members" without realizing that this claim upsets the whole groundwork of the present redistribution proposals and that if we want to upset it, it is up to us to propose something better that will command general assent. If we are not able to tackle this job, and do it thoroughly, we might realize that repeating our claim is simply employing time and energy that could be used to better purpose, and that we shall only be disappointed at the end, and that, surely is not worth while, whatever little political scores it gives you on the way. I am quite aware that I might become the most popular man in the Duchy by running a campaign that Cornwall is of such special importance that there must be no reduction of the present membership. But this is not a time for bothering about personal popularity. It's a time for facing up to facts, and the facts are that we must either accept the present proposals or work out a new system more likely to be generally approved.

F.D. Acland

[1] The Representation of the People Act of 1918, which was based on the recommendations of the Speaker's Conference, established the principle that constituencies should be equal in terms of population. However, Butler and Sloman in *British Political Facts 1900–1979* point out that 'Wales, Scotland and Ireland were allowed to retain disproportionate numbers of seats' (p. 227). In 1917 the Cornish opponents of redistribution claimed that Cornwall was equally entitled to an exemption.

DRO, 1148 M/671

FRANCIS ACLAND TO ELEANOR ACLAND

June 1917

Montagu told me yesterday that he thought the Reconst[ructio]n Committee would soon be disbanded, and be superseded by a Reconst[ructio]n Department (presumably with himself in charge[1]). He said that I should be asked to become one of its officers taking charge of all agricultural questions. This ought to suit me very well – and I'm happy about it. How soon it will happen & whether it will knock out the idea of a holiday in September I don't know. I am going to agree generally and ask for details. I've heard from Heath who agrees with me that I ought not to do any steady work in the division until the new boundaries are settled – and that it is important that I should do it then if I can settle terms which would be mutually satisfactory. This means that I shall not go in September for boundaries wont be settled by then; and it will be difficult to get any time later. That will have to look after itself.

[1.] In the event Montagu became Secretary of State for India in July 1917 and the Reconstruction portfolio went to Christopher Addison.

DRO, 1148 M/672

FRANCIS ACLAND TO ELEANOR ACLAND

8 August 1917

I've done very little today except go to Wimbledon to see [Uncle] Charles. I found him up but very weak and depressed though getting better; and very pessimistic about all public affairs. I got off my speech somehow. Not very good. It displeased Prothero because I criticised, & displeased my own people because I praised. Sir George Reid the Australian[1] said it was excellent so it may have had good points and I got in some strong things about labour . . . If Addison[2] would settle whether he wants me or not it would be a relief.

[1.] Sir George Reid (1845–1918) was Prime Minister of New South Wales 1894–99 and Prime Minister of Australia 1904–05. He was appointed as the first high commissioner in London in 1910 and was a popular speaker during the First World War. In 1916 he was returned unopposed as the 'Non Party Empire' candidate for the London seat of St George, Hanover Square.
[2.] Christopher Addison (1869–1951) was Minister for Reconstruction 1917–19. He was Liberal (then Lloyd George Liberal) MP for Hoxton 1910–22, Minister of Munitions 1916–17, President of the Local Government Board 1919–21 and Minster of Health 1919–21. Labour MP for Swindon 1929–31 and 1934–5 and Minister of Agriculture 1930–31. Created Lord Addison in 1937 and Leader of the House of Lords 1945–51.

DRO, 1148 M/677

FRANCIS ACLAND TO ELEANOR ACLAND

1917

I didn't write yesterday. I spent the day in copying out the notes of the speech that I want to get off on Friday, getting them typed, & sending a copy to Bonar Law[1], and to Spender, & to Montagu who is to move an amendment to Collins' motion which will I hope get things onto practical lines. It was a very jolly letter that I got from you when I came back to dinner before going to vote on P[roportional]. R[epresentation]. Poor old Lord Courtney[2] was in the gallery who has worked at the thing for 32 years but still had a majority of 32 against him. I thought the House showed great stupidity. I'm not at all disinclined to chuck politics but the every now and then occurrence of chances to be useful such as I have had as Ch[airma]n of the Afforest[atio]n Com[itt]ee and as I may have at Reconstr[uction] in Agriculture make it not easy to make up one's mind.

A good deal will depend on whether the new constituency will make finances possible & will elect me. Both quite doubtful I think.

I still believe the war will end this summer or autumn & therefore that we should not try to go to Sprydon[3] till its over.

[1.] Andrew Bonar Law (1858–1923) was the Conservative MP for Glasgow Blackfriars 1900–06, Dulwich 1906–December 1910, Bootle 1911–18 and Glasgow Central 1918–23. He was leader of the Conservative party 1911–21 and 1922–23, Secretary of State for Colonial Affairs 1915–16, Chancellor of the Exchequer 1916–19, Lord Privy Seal 1919–21 and Prime Minister 1922–23.

[2.] Leonard Henry Courtney (1832–1918) had been a leading advocate of proportional representation since the 1870s. He was Liberal (later Liberal Unionist) MP for Liskeard (1876–85) and Bodmin (1885–1900), Financial Secretary to the Treasury 1882–84 and Deputy Speaker 1886–92. Courtney returned to the Liberals in 1900 as a result of the Boer War and was created Baron Courtney of Penwith in 1906.

[3.] Sprydon was a Georgian House near Killerton that belonged to the Acland family and became the Devon home of Francis and Eleanor before inheriting Killerton.

DRO, 1148 M/777

FRANCIS ACLAND TO ELEANOR ACLAND

9 October 1917

A real wet day with a strong west wind that is making splendid waves on the big rock outside as I can see even from here. But I have to be at Camborne by 12.30 so shan't get a walk on the cliffs, . . . Post's not in yet so I haven't heard from you (will you by the way verify from my mother that father is 70 on the 13th). We had a "very great success" yesterday at Pool as we had had at Troon. We had a first rate working man to take us round and saw lots of miners & had them at our meeting – as nearly enthusiastic as this queer people can be at anything which appeals to their brains & not to their emotions. I find the old man's saying that I was not so select a [?] as he had expected makes a good story. I see that the *New Statesman* says that Ll[oyd]. G[eorge]. has determined to have a purely Ll[oyd]. G[eorge] election "vote of confidence in the Gov[ernmen]t" sort of business as soon as the new register can be made. Will he back me or Goldman[1] & if he backs Goldman will it do me good or harm. If the Labour men put up Eddy or Tangye I don't think we need be much afraid of them[2] – as the people here are such selfish souls that they'll think I can do more for them than an inexperienced man can do. They are an odd lot. If we were here every day for two years we could make something of them but it would take me all that to make them treat me just like a man. I shook hands with a fine lot of men who were mending the train line & had a word or two of empty chat and they were all so pleased as Punch; and I believe that in their present state of development the candidate who can shake hands with most of them would win. I believe if we can get an autograph letter to all the women voters as soon as the registers are published before any other party thinks of it we shall mop up the women's vote wholesale!

[1.] Goldman was originally planning to contest the new seat as a Conservative.
[2.] In the event the Labour party selected George Nicholls (see below) as its candidate.

DRO, 1148 M/678

FRANCIS ACLAND TO ELEANOR ACLAND

10 October 1917

What you say about giving up politics & going to Sprydon wants pondering.

I think that if U[ncle] C[harlie] would have a good agent there would be much to be said for it, but I feel that two years of butting my head against U[ncle] C[harlie] . . . would be about as bad as two years political work in Cornwall. Also if the best of the Liberals & Labour men would come out . . . against Ll[oyd] G[eorge] I should very much want to be in it, & should not easily be forgiven for standing aside till I saw which way the cat was going to jump. However if we let the house we wont let it beyond March so as to be free to clear out at Camborne if it seems the right thing to do. I'm not at all disinclined to say that if the miners will put forward a good miner I'll retire and support him – but there is no chance of their finding a good man or trusting him. It's lovely here today and I wish we were back in Cornwall with a long day before us on the cliffs . . . If there's an election next Spring & I'm beat which is very likely I should be all for standing aside for a bit but I don't think quite that I ought to withdraw now.

DRO, 1148 M/776

FRANCIS ACLAND TO ELEANOR ACLAND

12 October 1917

I haven't heard any aftermath of my Cornish doings yet, but no doubt the usual rumours are around all right. I think we did though manage for the first time to get into people's heads that we aren't high & mighty & un-approachable, and that's a very good thing done.

DRO, 1148 M/681

FRANCIS ACLAND TO ELEANOR ACLAND

30 October 1917

It's a queer time for us just now but I don't quite see being out of Parliament but I possess, as you do, somehow such a very large amount of general competence that I don't think I should for long be without pretty useful & honourable work.

DRO, 1148 M/682

FRANCIS ACLAND TO ELEANOR ACLAND

17 November 1917?

I have to wait here in case we reach Cornwall in the Schedules to the Reform Bill – not that there's anything much I want to say but that if every other Cornish member says something I must. . . . I'll send you the Hansard of last night's debate. I listened to Macdonald[1] & agreed to almost all he said & then to Balfour.[2] Balfour's right that there's no chance of Germany making any peace that we could accept now & that she hasn't stated what she wants anything like as definitely as we have, & that until she says something really definite about Belgium Poland & [Armenia?] we can't pretend that Alsace Lorraine blocks the way. But Macdonald & the rest are right that we ought to be & might be clearer than we have been, & might have encouraged the moderate Germans more than we have done. The point I stick to is that this gang of ours hasn't the imagination or the sympathy or democratic feeling to make the best of the position. Also of course there is a strong imperialistic gang in France & Italy & here who want the war to give them big new chances of exploiting the world to their own advantage. I'm not sure that we shan't want a good Russian revolution all round before things have any chance of settling down.

[1] James Ramsay MacDonald (1866–1937) was a leading member of the anti-war Union of Democratic Control and a former chairman of the Labour party. He went on to become the first Labour Prime Minister in 1924 and led a second government 1929–31. As leader of National Labour he was Prime Minister in the National Government 1931–35 and Lord President of the Council 1935–37.
[2] Sir Arthur James Balfour (1848–1930) was Conservative Prime Minister 1902–05 and a MP from 1874–1922. He returned to government as First Lord of the Admiralty 1915–16, Foreign Secretary 1916–19 and Lord President of the Council 1919–22 and 1925–29. Became Earl of Balfour in 1922.

DRO, 1148 M/683

FRANCIS ACLAND TO ELEANOR ACLAND

late 1917

Yesterday was a rush 10.15–11.30 conf[erence] with Father over land settlement (not much progress made) then conf[eren]ce with A[gricultural]

O[rganisation] S[ociety] organisers & lunch with them & back for more conf[eren]ce from which the main point arising is that I shall have the whole of the job of organising the allotment holders of the country onto me as chairman of the AOS allotments committee. I ought to select 40 new organisers, get out some first rate literature, arrange a first class system of trading, and get the Gov[ernmen]t to give as much security of tenure as is reasonable. It's about whole time work for three men! . . .

Then back in time to speak but with no time for dinner. You'll see the rest in the Times. A great argee bargee & Cave[1] dreadfully sticky about the [?] Speaker's Conference & Samuel [2] awfully timid. Runciman had to be prized off the bench like a limpet off a rock but we shall have a good chance of getting the thing through. It means I've got to write 16 letters to members getting them to turn up on Tuesday and telling them what to say. The Tory and Labour supporters left us dreadfully in the lurch but I think I can get them to make a better show on Tuesday. I've arranged with the NUWSS for a rain of telegrams to B[onar]. Law. The little pig Hayes Fisher[3] was trying to get Cave to refuse & we've turned the Local Gov[ernmen]t societies onto him, and onto the antis. If Cave will give us an open vote we shall win hands down. Northcliffe's letter![4] Isn't it damnable that a Br[itish] PM should put himself in a position to receive such a thing. Really Lord Reading[5] had to be sent out to America post haste to undo N[orthcliffe]'s muddles.

1. Sir George Cave (1856–1928) was Conservative MP for Kingston 1906–18. In 1915 he joined the Coalition as Secretary General and was appointed as Home Secretary by Lloyd George in 1916. He was ennobled as Viscount Cave in 1918 and served as Lord Chancellor 1922–23 and 1924–28.
2. Sir Herbert Louis Samuel (1870–1963) was Liberal MP for Cleveland from 1902–18 and Darwen from 1929–35. He was Chancellor of the Duchy of Lancaster 1909–10, Postmaster General 1910–14 and 1915–16, President of the Board of Local Government 1914–15 and Home Secretary 1916 and 1931–2. He was leader of the Liberal party 1931–35 and became Viscount Samuel in 1937.
3. William Hayes Fisher (1853–1920) was Conservative MP for Fulham 1885–1906 and January 1910–18. He was Financial Secretary to the Treasury 1902–03, Parliamentary Secretary to the Local Government Board 1915–17, President of the Local Government Board 1917–18 and Chancellor of the Duchy of Lancaster 1918–19. Became Baron Downham in 1918.
4. Alfred Charles William Harmsworth (1865–1922) was a leading newspaper proprietor. He became Baron Northcliffe in 1905 and he was appointed as head of the British War Mission to the USA in 1917. By this time, however, there was growing concern over his erratic behaviour and his claims to influence government policy.
5. Sir Rufus Daniel Isaacs (1860–1935) was Liberal MP for Reading 1904–13, Solicitor General 1910, Attorney General 1910–13, Lord Chief Justice 1913–21, Special Ambassador to USA 1918–19 and Foreign Secretary 1931. He was created Baron Reading in 1914 and Marquis of Reading in 1926.

DRO, 1148 M/686

FRANCIS ACLAND TO ELEANOR ACLAND

late 1917

Ll[oyd] G[eorge]'s speech made me wet half my pocket handkerchief with tears but I was up in the gallery and no one saw me mopping away. I think my waterworks turn on very easily, but we are a very unemotional race for I couldn't see anyone else even blowing his nose. The fishermen trawler captain with both his legs shot off who said "throw the confidential instructions overboard & throw me after them" was as good as Benbow. Asquith really knew that Ll[oyd] G[eorge] had got himself in to a bad hole having agreed to one thing with the Cabinet & to another with the French, and A[squith]. surely played the patriotic game, perhaps too much in giving them help to get out.

DRO, 1148 M/687

FRANCIS ACLAND TO ELEANOR ACLAND

November 1917

I really think the Liberal party is dead & that one will simply have to think of men & policies after the war – not of parties. I think the ex-Cabinet ministers might have done more than they have done in working out policies on social questions & that sort of thing (for instance Asquith should have made a very big protest against dropping the Ed[ucatio]n Bill) but it would have been very difficult to do without being violently attacked – "You say let us all unite and get on with the war but really you're taking advantage of the Gov[ernmen]t being hard at work to undermine them & disturb the country & direct it from working at the war". It'll be a queer time & the politicians who, like us, have a chance of doing something else & some capacity for doing it will be the happiest.

I didn't tell you that Churchill[1] had asked me to be Chairman of his Com[mitt]ee which arbitrates upon & decides all questions of women's employ[men]t in the Ministry of Munitions & as his adviser on all women's questions. I could not combine it with the Wages B[oar]d work, so had to say 'no'.

I had a busy day yesterday & "did good" ending with a drill. . . . One of the recalcitrant West Country farmers says "You tell me that 10/– isn't enough for my man so I've sacked him though he wants to stay. Is that right?" Not an easy letter to answer. Uncle Charlie tells me that the man he recommended most strongly to go on the Ag'[ricultural] Wages B[oar]d as representing the labourers has never been a real ag'[ricultural] lab'[ourer] in his life. So he wont do – & that's that.

Camborne wants more money to pay for my meetings – which is what one would expect. I go to see Fred Carkeek[2] again this afternoon & shall I suppose get him another 4/6 basket of apples.

[1] Winston Churchill (1874–1965) was Minister of Munitions at this time. Originally a Conservative he was a rising star of the Liberal government 1905–15 but was criticised for the Dardanelles fiasco in 1915. Returning to office under Lloyd George he subsequently became Secretary of State for War & Air 1919–21 and the Colonies 1921–22. After rejoining the Conservatives he was Chancellor of the Exchequer 1924–29 and Prime Minister 1940–45 and 1951–55.

[2] Presumably Frederick Carkeek who was a son of Sir Arthur and Lady Carkeek.

DRO, 1148 M/28

RAY STRACHEY[1] TO FRANCIS ACLAND

21 November 1917

Dear Mr Acland,

I know that it is unnecessary to send you the formal thanks of our Committee for all the work you have done for women, but nevertheless you must allow me to do so because my Committee feel such sincere gratitude to you. If I may, I should like to add my personal thanks. One of the difficulties of being Parliamentary Secretary to an organisation like this is that you have to deal with Members of Parliament who, although they agree and approve of what you want, are very unwilling to take any trouble or put themselves to any inconvenience to forward it, and you have always been such a delightful exception to this rule that I must thank you for it.

I want also to congratulate you on your stage management; it was so perfectly successful yesterday that it could not have been improved.

Yours sincerely,
Ray Strachey

[1] Mrs Ray Strachey, nee Costelloe (1887–1940) was a pre-war suffragist and became

Parliamentary Secretary of the National Union of Women's Suffrage Societies in 1915. She was the Independent parliamentary candidate for Brentford & Chiswick 1918–23.

DRO, 1148 M/689

FRANCIS ACLAND TO ELEANOR ACLAND

December 1917

And the House of Commons is bound to be interesting & may be exciting. There must be a hardening out on one side or other over this Lansdowne letter[1] and what will follow from it. I shouldn't wonder if those who back the letter, as I certainly must, would be violently unpopular & much attacked in the Press. The word has evidently got round the Gov[ermen]t papers for opposition to the letter . . . The Observer is disgusting. They show not the slightest trace of realising what seems to me the central fact, that the war can only end if the people on both sides who want security for the future rather than triumph for the moment can get control in their different countries & then get together. I wish Grey and Asquith & Henderson[2] would <u>now</u> come out and say ditto to Lansdowne, now when its most unpopular & inopportune & all the rest of it. I wonder what they think! I suppose that they can't try to force an election till there's a new register & that by mid summer when we can have an election there will be more chance of their carrying it if they let the logic of facts soak into peoples minds for a bit, and don't give Jingoes too much chance of saying that they want to knuckle under to Germany at the moment when Germany seems strongest. This is on the assumption that they wont come out strong now. I'd like to ask Garvin[3] whether he really wants to encourage the Junkers & keep them on top. I suppose he'd say – I do – & I want to smash them on the field & then be able to dictate terms, & I prefer a "victory" that way with all its consequences of Germany simply working for vengeance than to have a "negotiated" peace on the basis of every person in every nation realising the utter disaster of war & caring more tremendously about making it impossible in future than about anything else in their lives. All the papers assume that Lansdowne is proposing immediate knuckling under to Germany. All he really proposes is that when Germany is willing to make certain withdrawals & territorial concessions which in the light of what has happened in Russia we ought to be willing to restate & to state plainly she should know that we are willing to negotiate on the basis that she will remain a free nation. I wish you were here & we could jaw it all out. I feel that the press control by hard unimaginable brutes is a most fearful evil for us, & that there's no one in the Gov[ermen]t big enough to see that we keep big and [?] & free. Also I'm uncomfortable in myself for the moment to say anything in public the answer will be why don't y<u>ou</u> fight & even though there's a v[ery]. good answer to that any answer to that question is difficult.

1. Refers to a letter by the Marquis of Lansdowne (see above) that was published in the *Daily Telegraph* on 29 November 1917. Lansdowne called for a redefinition of the country's war aims and advocated a negotiated peace settlement with Germany. His views were criticised by pro-Lloyd George newspapers but warmly welcomed by opponents of the government.
2. Arthur Henderson (1863–1935) was Chairman of the Labour parliamentary party 1908–10 and 1914–17. He served as President of the Board of Education 1915–16, Paymaster General 1916, member of the War Cabinet 1916–17, Home Secretary 1924 and Foreign Secretary 1929–31. In 1918 he played a key role in the development of the party's organisation and the adoption of a socialist programme.
3. James Louis Garvin (1868–1947) was editor of the *Observer*. Before the war he had campaigned for rearmament against Germany and was a staunch supporter of the Lloyd George government. After the war, however, he emerged as a supporter of the League of Nations and called for a fair peace settlement with Germany.

DRO, 1148 M/697

FRANCIS ACLAND TO ELEANOR ACLAND

December 1917

Nothing has happened except that Winston [Churchill] is going to see that those . . . S[outh]. Crofty miners get a substantial rise. They never asked who they might give a war bonus! I sent you some more Ll[oyd].G[eorge] stuff that is very interesting. I am much distressed at the apparent incompetence of the Gov[ernmen]t. to take wise action for I believe more than ever that peace this year is possible.

DRO, 1148 M/698

FRANCIS ACLAND TO ELEANOR ACLAND

Monday afternoon, December 1917

I'm just going off to the House to hear Asquith & Ll[oyd]. G[eorge]. I think it'll be a tame affair for A[squith is] too much of a gentleman to hit hard & Ll[oyd].G[eorge] will explain that nothing is really intended that anyone can object to. The real objectionableness of the whole thing – the disparagement of our work in Flanders, – the deliberate attempt to force Robertson[1] to resign, the encouragement to the Germans from our showing how rattled we are, and the attempt at self glorification over Ll[oyd]. G[eorge]'s absurdly amateur ideas of strategy wont get touched on I expect. Charles Harris[2] says the desire to oust Robertson is at the bottom of it all. It's the Henderson business[3] over again. Why can't the man proceed by direct methods. If he could only believe that one of the people whom the nation as a whole are likely to trust really want to beat him in the same caddish way that he has beaten others – so that he needn't really be constantly throwing out clouds of ink & escaping through them like a cuttlefish – the Government of the country and its peace of mind would really get on much better.

[1] Lieutenant General William Robertson (1860–1933) was Chief of the Imperial General Staff. He disagreed with Lloyd George's view on the need to develop the Eastern Front and was eventually forced to resign in February 1918. In 1919 he was made a baronet and became a Field Marshal in the following year.
[2] Presumably Charles Harris, a civil servant at the War Office, referred to earlier.
[3] Refers to the 'doormat' incident in August 1917 when Arthur Henderson had been forced to wait outside the Cabinet Room while the other members of Lloyd George's administration discussed whether he should be allowed to attend an international socialist conference in Stockholm. Henderson promptly resigned from the cabinet.

DRO, 1148 M/699

FRANCIS ACLAND TO ELEANOR ACLAND

late 1917

Dearest,
I'm in the dumps about the whole thing now because we only got 30 at

the meeting at Redruth yesterday out of 200 cards sent out. I think the Labour people have sent word round to the working men that they're not to come, and they feel proud of staying away. At nine meetings I've had under 300 people & I doubt if one could pick out nine villages in Yorks or Lancs where I should have had such a poor attendance.

However – The great news is that we are not to be fastened onto Falmouth after all. We remain the Camborne division, and a string of rural parishes right round us are joined on including the borough of Helston. It's a tall bit of country with nothing picturesque about it except the names of the places Perranarworthal, Stithians, Mabe, Constantine, Breage, Carleen, [Burras?], Penhalveor, Perranzabuloe, Tregavethan. There will be very few miners or other organised workmen & it will really be a struggle between the squires & parsons & ourselves as to who can get the women. I feel awfully inclined – as just now – to say that I won't go on with it because of the utter lack of any interest by the people, but I suppose it would be cowardly. . . . I got an hour on the cliffs yesterday morning & saw fine waves but the tide was going out & they weren't shooting up much anywhere.

DRO, 1148 M/725

FRANCIS ACLAND TO ELEANOR ACLAND

1917?

I had quite a good meeting to finish up with at Lanner. Half a dozen men were really interested in the future of the world & though they mostly took the line of keeping Germany permanently crushed it was quite a sign of grace to find any interest in anything except what they could get for themselves. I spent the rest of the day seeing people in Redruth & Camborne & discussing the reshuffle of areas & the labour candidate.

If you could spare some time to write a line to Lady Carkeek saying you were sorry to learn that she and Sir Arthur were on the sick list it would be a graceful act. I went on Sunday evening to a Wesleyan Chapel service with C.V. Thomas which he took. I quite enjoyed it. The choir sang heartily. He preached & prayed well, and it was simple and impressive.

DRO, 1148 M/734

FRANCIS ACLAND TO ELEANOR ACLAND

1918

I must start to cycle on to Redruth at 12.30 & must see the sea first. Goodish meeting last night, but small. All very well. No letter from you expected or rec[eive]d.

DRO, 1148 M/735

FRANCIS ACLAND TO ELEANOR ACLAND

2 January 1918

The Bolsheviks[1] seem to have much method in their madness and I admire their audacity & don't see what the Germans can say. I hope we aren't going to be fools about it. If we keep steady & just say "We are quite willing to accept no annexations or indemnities provided it means that places like Poland & R.L. shall have the right after being evacuated to decide their own future, and provided we don't just go back to the old "balance of power" but form a league of nations with mutual disarmament to make it a reality – we should pip the Germans & yet keep the sympathy of the Russians.

I hear that we are going to bring an expedition from Mesopotamia to the Caucasus to link up with the Cossacks against Turkey. It strikes me as a very odd ramp indeed.

I've had a ten to six day at committees & Gov[ernmen]t offices & have enjoyed it, & got hold of old ropes again. And it has turned warmer so life is quite tolerable. Tell U[ncle] C[harlie] that Selborne told me he thought the businesslike thing would be to offer him the normal rate given by the B & W Publication Dept for his article though he was not sure whether he would take it as the article was a short one which had not cost him much time or work.

I lunched at the Club & weighed myself afterwards with great expectations after all the fine fat feeding. I'd gone down 21lbs! Never try to fatten FDA – it can't be done!

[1.] Lenin and his Bolshevik supporters had removed Alexander Kerensky's Provisional Government following a second Russian revolution in October 1917.

Negotiations for a peace treaty with Germany had commenced in December but it was not until 3 March 1918 that the Russian delegation led by Leon Trotsky ceded territories like Poland and the Ukraine under the terms of the Treaty of Brest Litovsk.

DRO, 1148 M/736

FRANCIS ACLAND TO ELEANOR ACLAND

4 January 1918

A day of agr[icultural] wages committees – disputes with the labour men most of this morning on the compos[itio]n of the District Wages Committees – & a breaking ground on rents this aft[ernoo]n on a comm[itt]ee I'm chairman of. This went fairly well but its savagely difficult.

I've just been dining with Maisie[1] – Walter[2] out. Were both going through a v[ery]. cold fit about his honour. I think the B[ritish].E[mpire]. order is going to be made very cheap, & that all honours are becoming more & more vile & that gradually men will more & more follow Galsworthy's[3] line of refusing them & that Walter has a g[rea]t chance of helping to set a good fashion. Maisie tries to think that a knighthood stills means a dedication to follow noble ideals, but she knows it doesn't & that Walter by taking it puts himself in a way alongside of the worst Hardy St bedside barts, & not being an Imperialist she doesn't like the E[mpire]. part of it. But she also knows that Walter feels that he'd like his war work recognised, specially as he's stuck to being a civilian & therefore had no chance of getting distinguished as a soldier – and she sympathises with this feeling.

Walter's argument mainly is that he was given no chance for Ll[oyd]. G[eorge]'s letter simply said that the king had approved. That won't wash – for Ll[oyd].G[eorge] has no right to notify in that way, he ought to ask men, & anyone can ask that his name may be withdrawn from the list which has been app[rove]d by H[is] M[ajesty], even if Ll[oyd] G[eorge] intimates the thing in a way that he has no business to.

[1.] Mary Francis 'Maisie' Cropper was Eleanor's sister. She married Walter Fletcher in 1904.
[2.] Sir Walter Morley Fletcher (1873–1933) was a noted physiologist and medical administrator. He became secretary of the Medical Research Committee in 1914 and was awarded the title of K.B.E. (Knight Commander of the Order of the British Empire) in 1918. Fletcher was largely responsible for the creation of the Medical Research Council in 1920.
[3.] John Galsworthy (1867–1933) was a prominent novelist and playwright. His

works include *The Forsyte Saga* and *Strife*. The latter work, written in 1909, is concerned with a strike at a Cornish tin mine and reflects his personal interest in the South West since his family came from the Plymouth area. His radical stand on issues ranging from penal reform to the House of Lords led him to refuse the offer of a knighthood in 1918.

———————

DRO, 1148 M/740

FRANCIS ACLAND TO ELEANOR ACLAND

4 January 1918

Ed[ucatio]n Com[mittee] today – & the work is getting on well. This will be our last meeting, and I shall be pleased with our report, though I haven't had very much to do with it. But the members like me and think me useful. All I really do is to provoke them to think clearly & to say what they really mean, which is just as necessary with the clear thinking scientific men that we have here as with any other sort.

The real thing with the KBE, as you say, is that Walter is a bit of a snob and loves it. There has never been one chance in 100 that he would refuse, and he doesn't really rate Maisie's objection very high. But Maisie does genuinely object, for she's a real christian & democrat and not an imperialist, and it will handicap her in many ways quite a lot, for which I am sorry. She was very much encouraged by your letter.

I've booked myself to talk about Foreign Affairs and the League of Nations Syllabus. British Foreign Policy before the war – was the war inevitable? – Democratic control. Essentials of a settlement. The implications of a League of Nations – Free trade as a basis for common economic action – Disarmament. Its really about three hours talk but I shall try at first to get it into one.

———————

DRO, 1148 M/743

FRANCIS ACLAND TO ELEANOR ACLAND

18 January 1918

Horribly negative Ll[oyd].G[eorge]'s speech is. He says that a League of Nations, disarmament and a solemn covenant are the right policy after the war in one place but he almost jeers at them elsewhere. There is nothing at all to set these up as great shining pinnacles to aim at. The pinnacle is "punishment". Horrible!

I've written a tiny note to the W[estminster].G[azette]. calling att[entio]n to the announcement that racing is to be [illegible] in the next columns of the Times to Ll[oyd].G[eorge]'s appeal to us to economise & to give up the things which are not essential to victory. They are an unimaginative set! Suppose instead there had been a statement of 'no racing, luxury restaurants closed etc', what a difference it would have made in the practical effect of the speech. . . . Yesterday I mostly fussed about forestry. Addison has been hatching a scheme which would really set things going – a new central body. £6,000,000 to spend – a definite 20 year planting programme to accomplish. Lovat[1] is opposing it & Selborne inclined to back him because its not all we asked for in our report & they are both booming about like mad bumble bees. And, as I see it, if they don't stop booming they'll get no scheme at all. So as you can imagine long talks to Vaughan Nash[2] etc, & then long letters to Selborne & Shirley Maxwell. The report will be published in the coming week.

[1.] Presumably Simon Joseph Fraser (1871–1933) who inherited the title of Baron Lovat in 1887 and had served as an army officer since the 1890s. During the First World War he was Director of Forestry on the Western Front. He was also the first chairman of the Forestry Commission 1919–27 and under secretary of state for the Dominions 1927–28.

[2.] Vaughan Nash (1861–1932) was secretary of the Ministry of Reconstruction 1917–19. He had previously served as private secretary to two Liberal Prime Ministers, Asquith and Sir Henry Campbell Bannerman, and was vice-chairman of the Development Commission 1912–29.

DRO, 1148 M/747

FRANCIS ACLAND TO ELEANOR ACLAND

5 February 1918

We've just beat P[roportional]. R[epresentation]. for good – & once more put in the alternative vote[1] though only in boroughs by 1 vote. I sh[oul]d think it is the first time on record that a thing has twice over been carried in the Commons by 1. I voted for P.R. & for the alternative of course. I think not having the Alternative may make me less easy to dislodge in Camborne for one will be able to use the rotten argument "don't vote

Labour for fear of letting the Tory in". But it's difficult to say how anything will go.

1. The Speaker's Conference had recommended a combination of Proportional Representation (in this case the Single Transferable Vote system) and the Alternative Vote. The latter system would have retained individual constituencies with voters ranking candidates in order of preference and removing the possibility of a member being elected on a minority vote.

DRO, 1148 M/749

FRANCIS ACLAND TO ELEANOR ACLAND

21 February 1918

We've been bow-wow-wowing here for two hours revising a page of type of one report on the demobilisation of Civil war workers. Miss Lawrence[1] and Dr Marion Philips[2] & Mallon[3] & I talk in favour of the workers (chiefly Miss Lawrence) & two employers Majoribanks & Jordine for the other side, & various officials from the Ministry of Munitions & Ministry of Labour etc. put us right all the time.

The worst sort of man is he who when both sides have agreed on something as a compromise which we both agree to though neither like – asks – when we've gone on to the next subject – what exactly was the wording agreed to & then because of a tiny point proposes to leave it all out. Its all about a suggestion to give munition workers a fortnight's holiday somehow after demobilization. The employers are extraordinarily stiff in opposing anything of the sort, though they will all individually say that they need at least a month themselves to recover from war. They entirely refuse to take a broad view that there would be more general friendliness & less unrest, &, as education develops, more intelligent work if there were rather more holiday.

1. Susan Lawrence (1871–1947) was a member of the Ministry of Reconstruction committee on employer-employee relations. After defecting from the Conservatives in 1912 she became a Labour member of London County Council and Labour MP for East Ham North 1923–24 and 1926–31. She was private secretary at the Board of Education 1923–24 and parliamentary secretary at the Ministry of Health 1929–31.
2. Dr Marion Philips (1881–1932) served on the Women's Advisory Committee of the Ministry of Reconstruction. She obtained a research scholarship at the London

School of Economics in 1904 and was associated with the Women's Trade Union League. After the war she became Chief Woman Officer of the Labour party and was Labour MP for Sunderland 1929–31.

3. James Joseph Mallon (1874–1961) served on a number of government committees concerned with reconstruction and wartime profiteering. He had emerged as a prominent campaigner for social reform in the previous decade and was secretary of the National League to Establish a Minimum Wage. In 1918 he failed to win Saffron Walden for Labour and was again unsuccessful at Watford in 1922 and 1923.

———————

Liskeard Liberal Democrat Office (LLDO hereafter), collection of Bodmin Liberal Association letters from the First World War

C.A. MILLMAN[1] TO FRANCIS ACLAND

Liberal Club, Liskeard, 21 February 1918

Strictly Confidential

Dear Mr Acland,

I was sorry that I was unable to meet you at the station today as you passed through, and am still more sorry that I shall not be able to see you in town on Friday as arranged. But I have had a rather sharp attack of la grippe and do not feel at all well enough to journey up and back in this uncertain weather. May I say that I have read your war speeches at Camborne and Redruth with much pleasure and complete agreement. I only wish the responsible members of the Government would speak in the same way and advance the same aims with similar moderation. The situation is enough to make one despair.

I wanted to see you on a most important matter which I must ask you to treat in the strictest confidence, and I know you well enough to know that you will do so. In the first place let me say that what I have to say in the matter I desire to bring to your notice is purely unofficial and unauthoritative. Mr Isaac Foot [2], who is at present our candidate, and a better candidate no constituency could possibly wish for, intimated to me quite recently when we were discussing the future that situated as he was, with a large and growing legal practice, with his partner away on service, and the future of six young children to consider, it would mean the ruin of his business if he were to contest the division and succeed. Anxious as he is to stand by the division and perfectly willing to fight if the way was clear, he says it is really impossible under present conditions. He very much wishes to stand at the next election, but would prefer to stand for a constituency in which there would be no chance of his being returned. We are thus compelled, in view of an Election this year, to move quietly with a view to finding a suitable candidate. I have had a talk with our Hon Secretary on the matter and we hit upon you as being one who would suit us down to the ground if you were at liberty. May I ask you if you are fully and irretrievably committed to the Mining Division, or would you be prepared to consider a formal and official invitation to become the candidate for this division, should such an invitation be sent you?

I am certain you would be more at home here than in your present division, and you would not be called upon to pay more than one half of the amount you at present pay for the privilege of representing the Camborne division, which I understand is £300 per annum. Please let me know what you think about this suggestion, but do not mention the matter to anyone, as no one knows anything about the matter save Mr J.A. Elliott, solicitor of Liskeard and Plymouth, who is the Hon. Secretary of our Association.

With kind regards,
Yours faithfully,
C.A. Millman

[1.] C.A. Millman was the Liberal agent for Bodmin. In 1919 he defected to the Labour party and was briefly prospective parliamentary candidate for North Cornwall. He was Labour agent for Penryn & Falmouth in 1922.
[2.] Isaac Foot (1880–1960) was Liberal MP for Bodmin 1922–24 and 1929–35. His advocacy of nonconformist causes like temperance meant that he was popular with local Methodists. He was Minister of Mines 1931–32, Vice-President of the Methodist conference 1937–38 and Lord Mayor of Plymouth in 1945. In 1937 he became a member of the Privy Council.

DRO, 1148 M/754

FRANCIS ACLAND TO ELEANOR ACLAND

1918

Why (you see the rotten state of my mind) did the W[omen's].L[iberal]. Fed[eration] refuse to let Mrs Asquith[1] come onto the platform with Asquith the other day? This is Gulland's talk & he said it gave great offence. I told him he must have got hold of that wrong – that you weren't small minded in that sort of way.

1. Margot Asquith, nee Tennant (1864–1945) became the second wife of Herbert Asquith in 1894. She was the daughter of Sir Charles Tennant, a Liberal MP. Her tactless approach apparently contributed to the divisions within the Liberal party.
2. John William Gulland (1864–1920) was Liberal MP for Dumfries Burghs 1906–18. He was a Junior Lord of the Treasury 1909–15 and Government Chief Whip 1915–16. Acted as Chief Whip of the Free Liberals 1916–18.

DRO, 1148 M/755

FRANCIS ACLAND TO ELEANOR ACLAND

1918

I must find out now what the War Office wants me to do for I can't settle down really steadily until I know. I think Charlie Harris will be able to get me an interview with the right man. Everything seems in an awful haze here. Gov[ermen]t has made an awful mistake I think about Ireland[1]. You can't drive those men. The bill even if forced through will give them no men, but if they c[ou]ld have given Home Rule with both hands, they'd have got splendid recruiting: & willing men train twice as quickly as unwilling.

DRO, 1148 M/758

FRANCIS ACLAND TO ELEANOR ACLAND

6 June 1918

Father with whom I had a successful – if scanty – dinner wanted me to tell you that he'd been much impressed with the way U[ncle]. C[harlie]. had tried to bring the labourers & farmers together in Broadclyst parish. He'd had both sides to tea separately – & then had been to see a farmer who was alleged to be underpaying a man – & had got things settled. All this father thought excellent as it is. I've got a wild scheme in my mind now – to arrange that Camborne shall be regarded as a Labour seat & for me not to stand there again, & to stand for the Tiverton division in which Sprydon is on a sort of independent radical ticket. I should be opposing a Coalition member & should no doubt have the whole force of the Gov[ernmen]t against me – but it would be rather fun. I might even get in, but I doubt.

DRO, 1148 M/759

FRANCIS ACLAND TO ELEANOR ACLAND

July 1918

I like the difficulty & the resignations – you may have seen in today's Times a statement I made about them. The difficulty is dreadful. A fairly good sub-committee after working for weeks has brought up a schedule which contains perfectly hopeless things, such as "all goods of a purely ornamental nature", "rods, nets etc", "educational" books to be at a higher figure than others, & I sat up till past two on the night before last getting out a paper drawing attention to all this & suggesting alternatives. I am amazed at the lack of quite ordinary elementary commonsense in the ordinary members of Parliament who are on my committee. They wont really give their minds to the thing with any high sense of public duty. How I would like sometimes a quiet walk around the Ellergreen garden with you to blow off steam.

LLDO, collection of Bodmin Liberal Association letters from the First World War

C.A. MILLMAN TO FRANCIS ACLAND

Liberal Club, Liskeard, 20 August 1918

Private and Confidential

Dear Mr Acland,

I intended writing you yesterday but was much too busy. I observed in yesterday's 'Mercury' a report to the effect that Mr George Nicholls[1] has accepted the invitation extended to him to become the Labour candidate for Camborne. If the report be correct how does that fit in with the statement made to you? I am disposed to accept it as an indication that steps are being taken to carry out the suggestion I made to you in a former letter. If this be so I should be glad to be informed.

I hardly know what to think about the rumours afloat regarding a General Election. Bearing in mind Mr Lloyd George's temperament and what I believe would be his desire to secure a renewed lease of power I should not be at all surprised if he were to make up his mind to risk an appeal to the country. A creature of impulse he might very easily be persuaded by his newly found friends to take the plunge.

If he does so where shall we stand and what shall we do as a party? I think we have surrendered too much already and made an excessive display of patriotic self restraint. We can go too far in that direction to our undoing. I am as much for winning the war as any fire eating jingo, but that does not require from me either the sacrifice of my political principles or the suppression of my convictions.

I know it is a very easy matter to criticise one's leaders for their silence and inactivity when the attention and energy of the nation should be concentrated on the supreme task of winning the war, but when that silence and inactivity are carried to the point of self-effacement it is time for the voice of criticism to make itself heard. No one can deny that our position as a party is being gradually undermined and our power for usefulness destroyed.

We look for a lead in the House of Commons and in the country but we look in vain. Meanwhile the Tories, accustomed to underhand methods, and the Labour party with a courage and purpose I admire and should much like to emulate, are preparing for the struggle which cannot long be delayed. We are daily losing supporters because we refuse to formulate a well-conceived programme. Never in our political history has a great political party been content to allow judgement to go against it by default as we seem to be willing to do.

I trust that ere it is too late something will be done to enable us to retrieve our position, which at the present moment is humiliating to the last degree. I refuse to believe that what is termed patriotism requires from us a measure of abnegation amounting almost to sacrifice. I am still hoping that it will be possible for you to come here. If you come I am absolutely confident we shall capture the seat.

With kind regards,
Yours faithfully,
C.A. Millman

[1.] George Nicholls (1864–1943) was Liberal MP for Northamptonshire North, 1906–January 1910 and chief organiser of the Allotment and Small Holders Section of the Agricultural Organisation Society. After contesting Camborne for the Labour party in 1918 he decided to rejoin the Liberals and fought a number of rural constituencies throughout England from 1922 to 1929.

LLDO, collection of Bodmin Liberal Association letters from the First World War

C.A. MILLMAN TO FRANCIS ACLAND

Liberal Club, Liskeard, 21 September 1918

Dear Mr Acland,

I gather from the Press that you propose coming to Cornwall soon for the purpose of addressing a series of meetings in your division. If this be so let me know the day and time you will pass through Liskeard and I will make a point of seeing you at the railway station. What is your view of a General Election at the end of the present or the beginning of next year? Personally I rather think it will come. L.G. seems to desire it and I presume he is in a position to gratify that desire. At any rate I do know that the Tory agent and his friends are making preparations for an early appeal to the country. May be they have received a hint from a responsible quarter.

If this be so we must prepare also. If an election comes the 'truce' goes by the board and we must fight for all we are worth. I do not desire a contest but I am not afraid of it.

With kind regards,
Yours faithfully,
C.A. Millman

DRO, 1148 M/760

FRANCIS ACLAND TO ELEANOR ACLAND

February 1918

After the Redruth meeting I've had a regular Cornish time. Utterly unable to find any sign that the people regard themselves as citizens or have any sort of duties in connection with carrying on the war. But the meetings have been carried through somehow and I've got off two pretty pacifist speeches without active opposition. There was a woman belonging to the Pankhurst gang[1] who tried to interrupt, but the audience objected to her not because of her point of view but as a stranger. Bain[2] the Tory Chairman spoke well moving a resolution tonight backing me up & particularly thanked me afterwards for daring to put a different point of view. But now half the audience held up their hands for the ordinary resolution & it was quite impossible to judge what they were thinking of, if anything. I send you my stuff in case you care to look it through. I'll get it when I come and we can talk it over. We had a jolly time this morning at Tehidy and on the north cliffs. There was a fair sea on & hundreds of gulls resting on the rocks and flying up and filling the air whenever we looked over. They were pairing but not nesting yet, and a raven, & flocks of jackdaws flying higher than the gulls. And all the gulls screamed. It started a drizzly day but gradually cleared and a good cold wind got up and I really like it. . . . I slept all the afternoon and that was pleasant but that and the cliffs were the only things I've liked. Bentinck[3] has made simple sensible speeches which have helped me because they've been just as League of Nations-y as mine – and therefore no one could say that I'd taken a party line. He's an awfully nice fellow and it has been v[ery] nice of him to come.

I don't think Carkeek liked my speech, but he hasn't yet said anything about it. I suppose I can be said to have gone out of my way to give Germans a good character.

I had an hour and a half talk with some miners before the meeting about their wages. I had pretty good news from Churchill to give them (though no increase has yet been given) so they were easy to do with, but it was awfully difficult to get them to understand that there could be any difficulty or that I couldn't have got them all a big increase straight off if I'd pleased.

[1.] A reference to the activities of the WSPU led by Emmeline Pankhurst (see above). In 1914 the suffragettes had decided to suspend their campaign for the duration of the war. Emmeline and her eldest daughter, Christabel Pankhurst (1880–1958), soon adopted a patriotic and right-wing approach to the war effort and in November 1917 the WSPU had been renamed as the Women's Party.

[2.] John H. Bain was Chairman of the Camborne Unionist Association.

[3.] Lord Henry Cavendish-Bentinck (1863–1931) was Conservative MP for Nottingham South 1895–1906 and again from January 1910–29.

DRO, 1148 M/765

FRANCIS ACLAND TO ELEANOR ACLAND

1918

I didn't tell you what the W[ar]. O[ffice]. man said. He was a good man & very sensible which is a marvel considering he was shot straight through both temples! He thought it perfectly obvious that I ought to stay as I was & clearly the W.O. will do nothing to alter things. He says the whole tendency of things is to reduce the age of officers sent abroad, & that the crisis makes no difference in that. But he said the National Service

Dep[artmen]t had some say in the matter & might have such as me sent through a special course at Cambridge (though he thought it unlikely) & he thought it pretty certain that I should be rejected by the doctors if anything of that sort came along. So I don't think we need fuss at all or let any possibilities affect our plans.

DRO, 1148 M/767

FRANCIS ACLAND TO ELEANOR ACLAND

1918

Its a dreadful time of fluctuation of news but always the Germans seem to gain a bit & we to lose. I wonder if Foch[1] has some big army that he uses a little of here & there to stop gaps when they get too bad – & will be able to use to make a big counterblow somewhere late. Its bad not knowing anything at all. Uncle Sydney says all the wounded officers are v[ery]. confident but that may just be our characteristic of not knowing when we're beat.

[1] Marshall Ferdinand Foch (1851–1929) was a leading French military strategist before the First World War and then commander of the Northern Army Group in 1915. He was appointed as Allied Commander-in-Chief in April 1918.

DRO, 1148 M/768

FRANCIS ACLAND TO ELEANOR ACLAND

Betws-y-Coed, 1918

It's jolly here. You'll be surprised to hear that I've been fishing. Yesterday afternoon I got 22 & today I got 50! All in about a mile of water. They were smallish but weighed over 12lbs altogether. I am believed to be one of the wonders of the world. Farmer got 18 today & is very pleased with himself. Its quite cold with a hard east wind & there's hardly any life in tree or field or water. But its jolly high healthy country and will do us both good. Tomorrow we are going to – fish! But I hope to be able to get Farmer away from the water either on Saturday or Sunday for a walk, as for the first time in my life I am getting to think I've nearly fished enough.

DRO, 1148 M/775

FRANCIS ACLAND TO ELEANOR ACLAND

1918

I've got to think out what to say to the Labour Party who have asked me to
come & talk to them about agriculture.

———————————

DRO, 1148 M/124

ELEANOR ACLAND TO FRANCIS ACLAND

1918

The Lloyd-George plot seems to me so vile & so likely to succeed in putting
in the Tories (leading thus bang up to Revolution) that I am driven to ask
even at this 11th hour whether it might just conceivably be your duty to
stand down? English politics are so utterly in the gutter that it seems to me
that some signal act of inequanmity is needed. Of course it would mean
throwing our whole weight into the Labour candidates' cause – otherwise
the result might be Peter[1]. It would utterly shock a section of your supporters
– but the less estimable section. I am convinced however that we could get
Nicholls in, & that we could make quite distinct headway towards creating
a real Lib.Lab coalition not merely for the constituency but for the whole
country. The part of the Labour world which is in the know & knows you
loves you & admires you already but you would gain a moral ascendancy
over the whole lot of them for good & all.

All quite too late! Address gone out to the Tommies. Send another –
speak out we could, which I feel all the time we can't now.

I'm activated partly by moral nausea at Carkeek's attitude.[2] Am I also
activated by love of doing rather a spectacular thing? Anyhow I feel as if I
mean it, as if I should feel cleaner & honester myself, & rid of the obscene
trouble of mind which muddles all my present speeches – But of course its
your show, & having once more gone into the fight I should go on backing
you up whatever you decide.

Only I can't help foreseeing how utterly miserable we should feel if
Peter got in. Of course I know you've got a sporting chance. If you hadn't,
to stand down wouldn't be anything specially fine.

There's the argument that you hooked yourself finally at the meeting of
the 500. But we didn't know then how bad the Northcliffe-Lloyd George

caucus was. Things have worsened considerably since then. There's the argument that if either you or Nicholls ought to stand down it should be Nicholls. It's his one chance, & you'll get plenty. I think you would be the Lib.Lab Foreign Secretary in 3 years time if you did it. And, what's more to the point, I don't think anything is going to count & weigh really in the appalling tussle this country has got to face except self sacrifice, even to the extent of being called, possibly, a coward by one's less good friends.

Anyhow, as I say, I'm at your service, old gentleman, & will put my heart into it for love of you, and as to my conscience – oh well – having said my say its appeased & willing to take your decision on trust. I can't help feeling though that we are a bit muffled & stifled in our speaking. I know I'm afraid of speaking out my whole mind on the international question.

The worst of the Ll[oyd]. George business is that it means not that he's a worm, but that Northcliffe is <u>so</u> strong that he has captured a man who isn't just a worm. To counteract Northcliffe & all the loathsomeness he stands for needs something absolutely heroic.

The Labour manifesto is splendid I think – far better on international points than the average Liberal dare be . . .

[1.] Captain G.F. Thomas-Peter had been the Unionist prospective parliamentary candidate for Camborne before 1914. He was stationed in India during the First World War and failed to get back to Britain in time to be nominated as the Conservative candidate.

[2.] Carkeek adopted an ambiguous stance towards the Lloyd George Coalition in the 1918 election. He stood as Liberal candidate for Penryn & Falmouth against an official Conservative nominee backed by the government but claimed that he was a supporter of Lloyd George.

———————————

DRO, 1148 M/733

FRANCIS ACLAND TO ELEANOR ACLAND

October 1918?

I've got to finish & tidy up, & get out to Redruth to see one of the Smiths [?] who is disgruntled about my attitude to Labour. He's a good employer in a factory & I shall be sorry if we lose him. Yesterday wasn't quite as nice as I've described it to g but I had a jolly hour or two in the afternoon. Tea with [?], a really pleasant man, cycled on to Redruth to supper with Carkeek after chapel & beastly wind coming back. Rain & wind again this morning, so I shan't be able to pick blackberries which are more wonderful than ever but have less taste.

I've just about had as much as I could have stood of this but I'm glad we did it. It will at any rate keep our consciences good when we're outed as I think we shall be – & in lots of ways it's been really jolly

---

Asquith papers, Bodleian Library, MS. Asquith 33, fol. 34

FRANCIS ACLAND TO HERBERT ASQUITH

Sprydoncote, Exeter, 29 December 1918

Dear Asquith,

The smash and the extraordinary injustice to yourself and your old colleagues is so great that it almost ceases to be a tragedy. I seem to be the only survivor of those who remained faithful to you who served under you in the first Coalition, and Lambert[1] and Benn[2] and I seem to be the only ex-ministers returned who would not say "Coalition". My return was rather a fluke for though I beat a good Labour man in a straight fight, I should not have won if the Tory candidate, who had not got back from India in time, had been put forward. I got some Tory support, but very little, for I kept it being absolutely independent, and lost some usually [loyal?] Liberal votes by doing it. I wish the seat were safe for Liberalism against all comers, for of course then I should be delighted to stand down so that you could take it but it is not. With a Tory standing Labour would win, for there is a solid block of Labour tin miners who care nothing about politics, but think that a Labour member would get their wages doubled.

I assume that those who survive of whom Benn, Hogge,[3] Arnold,[4] Collins,[5] Blake[6] & E.H.Young[7] seem likely to be the most useful, will have to try to pull themselves together until you and some of the others can get back. If I can be of any use in helping with this I am very much at your service, and would put my back into anything that you think I could usefully do. If, as seems possible, we ought to work closely with Labour I might be useful, as I am fairly well trusted by several of the Labour men owing to my work on the Agricultural Wages Board. But, as I think you know, I do not want in any way to push myself. I feel almost ashamed of having come through when all the good men have fallen.

Yours sincerely,

F.D. Acland

I come back to London this week for forestry work, & my address is 93 Bedford Gardens W8 (Park 4635).

[1] George Lambert (1866–1958) was Civil Lord of the Treasury 1905–15 and Liberal MP for South Molton 1891–1924 and 1929–45. He was a member of the Coalition Liberals 1919–22 and joined the Liberal Nationals in 1931. He became Viscount Lambert in 1945.

[2] William Wedgwood Benn (1877–1960) was Liberal MP for Tower Hamlets, St George's 1906–18 and Leith 1918–27. After defecting to Labour he represented Aberdeen North 1928–31 and Manchester Gorton 1937–42. He was Junior Lord of the Treasury 1910–15, Secretary of State for India 1929–31 and elevated to the peerage as Viscount Stansgate in 1942.

[3] James Myles Hogge (1873–1928) was Liberal MP for Edinburgh East 1912–24.

[4] Sydney Arnold (1878–1945) was Liberal MP for Holmfirth 1912–18 and Penistone 1918–21. On the Radical wing of the party he resigned in 1921 and joined the first Labour government in 1924 as Parliamentary Under-Secretary for the Colonies with a seat in the House of Lords as Lord Arnold. He was Paymaster General 1929–31.

[5] Sir Godfrey Pattison Collins (1875–1936) was Liberal MP for Greenock January 1910–36. After the 1918 election he took the Coalition Liberal whip but had apparently returned to the Independent Liberals by 1922. In 1931 he joined the Liberal Nationals and was Secretary of State for Scotland 1932–36.

[6] Sir Francis Blake (1856–1940) was Liberal MP for Berwick-Upon-Tweed 1916–22. After the 1918 election he decided to join the Coalition Liberals.

[7] Sir Edward Hilton Young (1879–1960) was Liberal MP for Norwich 1915–23 and 1924–26. Like Lambert, Collins and Blake he became a Coalition Liberal after the 1918 election and was Financial Secretary to the Treasury 1921–22. He represented Norwich as a Conservative from 1926–29 and Sevenoaks 1929–35. He was Minister of Health 1931–35 and became Lord Kennet in 1935.

Cornish Post, 04/01/19

FRANCIS ACLAND TO THE ELECTORS OF THE CAMBORNE DIVISION

Sprydoncote, Exeter, 30 December 1918

Ladies & Gentlemen –

I desire to thank the voters of the Camborne Division for having returned me once more as their Member of Parliament. I am sorry that an attack of bronchitis prevented me from being present when the poll was declared to thank them personally. I am proud of being, owing to their help, the only Liberal ex-Minister of the first Coalition Government who was returned free from pledges to the present Coalition. The nation has, I think, been extraordinarily unjust to the men who worked with Mr. Asquith and rendered such magnificent service to the State. History will I believe revise the verdict and time will quickly modify it. But at any rate the Camborne division did not think that hard public service and some independence of character were an absolute bar to the House of Commons and for this I am most grateful. In other ways I cannot be very proud of the result. The percentage of the electors who voted was the lowest of any Constituency in the West of England, probably, I think, the lowest in the whole Kingdom.[1] We polled 41 per cent (practically only four out of every ten possible voters), St Ives 51 per cent, Penryn and Falmouth 56 per cent, and Bodmin 69 per cent. I cannot justly feel proud of myself if I can induce only something less than 22 out of every hundred voters to vote for me, and the Liberal Party can feel little pride in their power of organisation which produces such a result in a Liberal seat. Clearly I must amend my ways or the Constituency theirs if there is to be that genuine partnership between constituency and member which ought to exist. I, at any rate, will do my best to learn a lesson.

But the lack of interest in the fight should in a way be helpful just now. The fight did not stir animosities, it should therefore not leave bad blood. It was claimed on insufficient evidence that the seat was a Labour seat. We now have the evidence, and know that it is not. If Labour, with all the attractions of novelty, cannot win at a time when independent Liberal stock stands so low as it does now, it must realise that it is not in any way in the position of predominant partner. It must therefore make the best of the position as it is. The Workers' Union has hitherto refused to let me try to help them on Labour questions. This was no doubt sound electioneering tactics, but we should forget tactics for a bit. Nothing now but the hardest possible work and the closest possible co-operation of all persons concerned can, I fear, prevent considerable disasters to our chief industries. Let us forget all differences and learn to work together. I am taking what steps I can to bring this about and I feel sure that all persons of goodwill towards the mining district will be doing the same.

May I once more thank those who voted for me for their extreme kindness in showing that they considered me worthy to represent them. Those who voted against me have that satisfaction of knowing that they performed a simple and elementary duty as citizens in a conscientious manner and on this I congratulate them.

I remain,
Yours faithfully,
F.D. Acland

[1.] The turnout in Camborne was not quite the lowest in Britain in 1918. It was certainly a poor result compared to the other county divisions and only seven other such seats had a lower turnout. The number of voters in borough seats like Lambeth, Kennington (29.7 per cent) and Birmingham, Deritend (30.7 per cent) was even lower and Camborne had the thirtieth lowest turnout in Britain.

DRO, 1148 M/784

FRANCIS ACLAND TO ELEANOR ACLAND

January 1919

I see in the papers that Sir D Maclean[1] is to lead the indep[endents]. If so well & good, he will be respectable – if not brilliant. It means that I lost my chance of doing it by being slack about all H[ouse]. of C[ommons]. things for the last two years. But I'm better at Committee work than at the House & not strong enough for both & I don't regret much having put myself out of the running. Maclean's leadership will not dispose of my chief point which is that five or six of us should work steadily and constantly in close touch with Labour, planning ahead for the ultimate success of a big democratic party.

Another mine has closed.[2] Things are going to be v[ery]. bleak in Cornwall. If I'd lost all the fault w[ou]ld have been put on Labour – now it will be put on me. I doubt whether [?] the half baked lot that we have to deal with I can push about enough to get the Government to save the position.

[1] Sir Donald Maclean (1864–1932) was Liberal MP for Bath 1900–10, Peebles & Selkirk 1910–22 and North Cornwall 1929–32. He was Deputy Chairman of Ways and Means 1911–19, chairman of the Independent Liberals 1919–22 and Secretary of State for Education 1931–32.

[2] A reference to the problems of the Cornish mining industry after the First World War. For further information on this subject see John Rowe, 'The Declining Years of Cornish Tin Mining' in J. Porter (ed.), *Education and Labour in the South West*, Exeter, 1975.

DRO, 1148 M/778

FRANCIS ACLAND TO ELEANOR ACLAND

Early 1919?

I'm getting a lot of good talk with my father which is useful. We both agree that the remnant or such of them as are not Lloyd Georgite as the Coalition will have to try to work more & more closely with Labour whatever Asquith may say or do. I think if we c[ou]ld get Simon[1] back & gather around him & he could make a working alliance with the non-

Gov[ernmen]t Labour men something would come of it.

I feel that it will be v[ery]. much a question of what each man does for himself. If we try to go on as a party nothing will come of it. The officials of the Liberal party will try to pretend that the two sections will some day reunite under Lloyd George and/or Asquith & will form a Government. They wont realise that Ll[oyd].G can't again lead a real Liberal party & that the Liberal p[arty] by whomever led is much too dead to make anything of itself as a real governing & directing force.

[1.] Sir John Simon (1873–1954) was regarded as Asquith's likely successor. He was Liberal (later Liberal National) MP for Walthamstow 1906–18 and Spen Valley 1922–40. Served as Attorney General 1913–15, Home Secretary 1915–16 & 1935–37, Foreign Secretary 1931–35, Chancellor of the Exchequer 1935–37 and Lord Chancellor 1940–45. Liberal National leader 1931–40 and was created Viscount Simon in 1940.

DRO, 1148 M/779

FRANCIS ACLAND TO ELEANOR ACLAND

February 1919?

I want to blow off too about politics and the beastliness of it. I am a fish out of water here, & practically have to begin everything over again at a time of life when fresh starts are not easy. The group is good natured & friendly but we are a weak lot in numbers & every other way. They were very pleased with my working out committees for them but we want about ten committees & have only about ten men whose work will be of any value. [Hilton?] has become Fishers' Parl[iamentary] secretary & will now just be a Government hanger on.[1] Last night I voted Labour because B Law's speech though v[ery] friendly & reasonable contained no suggestion of anything new or of any measures against profiteering. About 7 of us voted Labour, one or two voted for the Gov[ernmen]t & the rest abstained. This doesn't matter – we agree to differ & still work friendly [?] along but its not much of a start for a Radical group.

[1.] Possibly Edward Hilton-Young who was referred to earlier. He officially joined the government as Financial Secretary to the Treasury in April 1921.

DRO, 1148 M/780

FRANCIS ACLAND TO ELEANOR ACLAND

January 1919?

Asquith wanted to ask Lambert & me whether we objected to D[onald]. Maclean. As M[aclean]. & Asquith seemed both to be on right lines of running the group vigorously as a group in close co-operation with Labour. I said a hearty 'yes'. Lambert played the ass at great length – wanted us all to pretend we belonged to the Coalition & wait for some split & Asquith argued with him till he had to go . . . I've really established most friendly relations with Maclean, Gulland & Asquith. They welcome all my ideas of committees – helping the younger men etc – which I'm going to put on paper. Altogether I see for myself a position of usefulness – without too much responsibility – & am happy.

I told Lambert straight that if the group didn't get going & into close relations with Labour some of us would take that on ourselves unofficially, & Asquith warmly approved.

DRO, 1148 M/781

FRANCIS ACLAND TO ELEANOR ACLAND

Late January/February 1919?

That this meeting of Liberals take immediate steps to reorganise the Liberal Party and meanwhile appoint a Sessional Chairman (Hogge's motion).[1]

What are we? A dozen nonentities, half a dozen new members some of them quite good material, three or four quite wild & undependable men, three or four secretly or openly hostile to doing anything & only two or three left of any stability & experience & willingness & ability to work. Wow! but I don't like it. But I suppose its right to put my back into it. I do believe that if things go reasonably well we may make a tremendous difference on the country in the next few years. I wish I didn't hate the place quite so much & was better at all the little amenities of getting on with people I don't know. And I'd give anything for the power of making pretty good speeches about next to nothing. Things will shake down somehow I suppose, & it will be jolly interesting.

[1.] This was the motion presented by Hogge at the Independent Liberal meeting on 4 February 1919. It was intended as a challenge to the leadership of Asquith.

DRO, 1148 M/782

FRANCIS ACLAND TO ELEANOR ACLAND

Early 1919?

I'd hoped to get an after lunch sleep & get letters written before S[ydney]. Arnold came to tea; but he came early & found me asleep. We talked two hours – most jolly – wished you'd been there. He's a v[ery]. independent chap & won't join any group but we're very much on the same lines of wanting to work closely with Labour & to look well ahead for a fine democratic party for the future. He says that many of the best labour men want to welcome us as they feel nearer us than to some of their own Jingo colleagues, & that whatever they say they feel they must get more brains & general experience on their side before they can form a government. Arnold strongly approved of my idea of making something more for our group than just a machine for voting together from day to day – getting committees & study circles going on the big questions of the future. But, Lord, shall I have time for all that I'd like to do on those lines & for all I want to do & be & see at Sprydon.

I shan't of course but I must aim I think at cutting free from the most engrossing of the administrative jobs so as to have more time for House of Commons work.

Arnold says that most of the Coalition Lib[eral]s are pretending to be entirely unpledged & talking about meetings of the whole party[1] & keeping going the sacred principles of Liberalism. As if they hadn't broken every one of them by taking the ticket!

[1]. A reference to the manoeuvres of the Coalition Liberals in early 1919 who were concerned about the attempt to set up an independent Liberal group. On 5 February 1919 they held a meeting that was attended by Liberal MPs from both factions but eventually the Coalition Liberals were forced to form a separate parliamentary group under the chairmanship of Lambert.

DRO, 1148 M/785

FRANCIS ACLAND TO ELEANOR ACLAND

4 February 1919

Dearest,
. . . Then to the Free Liberal meeting. It was rather fun. Lambert who

was senior P[rivy] C[ouncillor] present moved me into the chair as he wanted to keep free to oppose what we wanted to do. We talked for over three hours though it seemed very black for forming a group at first the saner ones finally got on top and we settled to form one by about 16 votes to 4. There were two sets against it from opposite points of view. Lambert & Godfrey Collins who want to pretend that we are still all in the same boat [i.e. with the Coalition Liberals] & Wedgwood, S[ydney]. Arnold & Hogge who hate the old Lib[eral] party & don't want to have any sort of connection with it, & between the two of them (both very vocal) it seemed that we should get nothing done. There was a critical moment. Hogge had moved that we elect a sessional chairman pro forma as a peg for questions & discussion. Then when we'd all spoken I asked them to divide on it. He said it wasn't his motion & wanted to substitute 'that this meeting of Liberals take immediate steps to reorganise the Lib[eral] party & meanwhile appoints a sessional chairman'. That was dangerous for it w[ou]ld have been negatived. Then someone else wanted to move to form a group in 'order to reunite with the Co[alition]. Lib[eral]s. That was equally dangerous for it wouldn't have been carried either. So I boldly voted them both out of order & said that we must vote on what we had been discussing which was that we form a group & proceed to elect a sessional chairman & officers. I moved it. Sir J. McCallum[1] a dear old Scot seconded promptly, a crafty motion to adjourn (we sh[oul]d never have met again if we'd once adjourned) was defeated & my motion was put & carried. Hilton[2] didn't vote.

Well what next. Goodness knows. Its jolly difficult to be optimistic about our prospects.

[1] Sir John Mills McCallum (1847–1920) was the Liberal MP for Paisley 1906–20. His death in 1920 resulted in a by-election that enabled Asquith to return to the House of Commons.
[2] Presumably Edward Hilton Young who was mentioned earlier.

DRO, 1148 M/889

CHARLES TREVELYAN [1] TO ELEANOR ACLAND

24 May 1919

Dear Eleanor,

I have great sympathy with everyone's difficulties about party just now. All I really care about is that they should think rightly. I was delighted to see that the "bloated" one proposed a Levy on Capital[2] in the House. And I am not making any special effort to drag my friends over at once into the Labour Party. But I think most of you are likely to find yourselves there by the force of circumstances within the next few years. It is not that I think the leadership of the Labour Party good. It is not so from any point of view. But leadership matters much less there in the long run. All the leaders of all parties have proved themselves totally incapable of statesmanship during the war, and are still worse after it. It is only therefore by the growth of a new conscience and policy from Labour that partial right-eousness may be restored to the world. It may take a long time, a longer time than if there had been a great Liberal statesman. But the common people will manage to do it, and they will use the Labour party. The Liberal party has always depended on intellectual leadership. Its working class clientele was always led not leading. Now both the intellectual leadership is totally lacking, and what is far worse the moral. And the working class began to cease to vote Liberal at the last election and I am certain will never do so en masse again. That will again react and make the party more middle class, bourgeois, and eventually Whiggish than ever. Meanwhile the big world wants revolution – peaceful if possible.

Now the Labour Party can afford temporary bad leadership because it is democratic. I have just had an amusing evidence of that. This afternoon I went in to a Labour conference in Newcastle – 1000 delegates from Tyne Trade Unions. Adamson [3] came down and made, as he would, a stupid speech, wearying them with irrelevance and feebleness. No one except himself regarded him as leader. They were frankly bored. The moment his back was turned they went to business in a good series of vigorous speeches and a sharp discussion on "direct action" and whether there ought to be a strike against the Russian war and Conscription. Now in this same hall Asquith ten days before made his wretched address.[4] No condemnation of the wretched peace, no word about the shameless Russian war or the cruel blockade. What can the poor old Liberal party do? Nothing, nor will it. The rank and file won't move, because if they do they will at once join Labour as the most effective thing. The end of the war and the peace have smashed this Liberal party. They fought "a war to end war" and all the rest of it. Now they can't even bleat when it ends in for the most brutal militarist peace on record. You will soon find that in these days of absolutely grim seriousness you can't fight with people who only half agree, who never dare anything, and who have the war record of the Liberal leaders, [?] Conferences, secret treaties, condoning of the Russian war, blockade [?]

Parties are only methods of combining for political purposes. I have always been bored by the enthusiasm of the party man or woman. So I haven't found any great wrench in leaving the Liberal party. Nor do I expect much from the Labour party except that it will manage to evolve the organisation which will pretty soon get hold of the government, probably to make a horrid mess of it, but to undo almost in its stride the worst atrocities of the present regime.

In short I don't care where anyone works provided they work right. During the general election in Elland I made hundreds of votes for the official Labour candidate by my campaign, which he was totally incapable of making himself.[5] So it is a matter of small importance whether you or I or Kenworthy [6] or Snowden [7] make the public opinion which will soon crystallize into a working political machine. Incidentally I find the I.L.P.[8] quite enormously the most congenial organisation I have ever worked with – more camaraderie and less jealousy.

[1.] Sir Charles Philips Trevelyan (1870–1958) had been Liberal MP for Elland 1899–1918, a founder of the wartime Union of Democratic Control and Parliamentary Secretary to the Board of Education 1908–14. He was Labour MP for Newcastle-upon-Tyne Central 1922–31 and President of the Board of Education 1924 and 1929–31.

[2.] In 1919 there was growing support for the idea of reducing the wartime increase in the National Debt by means of a Levy on Capital. The Labour party was at the forefront of this campaign but there was some interest by both Independent and Coalition Liberals, including Winston Churchill.

[3.] William Adamson (1863–1936) was Labour MP for Fife West from December 1910–31 and chairman of the Labour parliamentary party 1917–21. He was Secretary of State for Scotland in 1924 and 1929–31.

[4.] Refers to a rather lethargic speech by Asquith at Newcastle on 15 May 1919 when he had failed to inspire his own supporters. For a discussion of this speech see Trevor Wilson, *The Downfall of the Liberal Party 1914–1935,* Collins, London, 1966, pp. 211–12.

[5.] In 1918 Trevelyan had contested the Yorkshire division of Elland as an Independent Labour candidate. He came fourth with just 5.6 per cent of the vote compared with 25.6 per cent for the official Labour candidate.

[6.] Hon. Joseph Montague Kenworthy (1886–1953) had been elected as the Liberal MP for Kingston-upon-Hull, Central in a by-election in March 1919. In 1926 he defected to Labour and continued to represent the seat until his defeat in 1931. He inherited the title of Lord Strabolgi in 1934.

[7.] Philip Snowden (1864–1937) was Labour MP for Blackburn 1906–18 and Colne Valley 1922–31. He was Chancellor of the Exchequer in 1924 and 1929–31. Remained as Chancellor of the Exchequer in the first National Government of 1931 and then Lord Privy Seal 1931–32. Created Viscount Snowden in 1931 and resigned from the government in 1932 over the introduction of tariffs.

[8.] The ILP (Independent Labour Party), which had been formed in 1893, was affiliated to the Labour party but maintained a separate identity by sponsoring its own candidates and advocating a more left-wing policy agenda. Growing differences with Labour meant that Trevelyan and his ILP colleagues, including Kate Spurrell at Camborne, were to fight the 1931 election as a separate party.

DRO, 1148 M/890

CHARLES TREVELYAN TO ELEANOR ACLAND

5 June 1919

Dear Eleanor,

I am very much pleased to find how much we agree. It would be far better for the Labour Party to be the "Socialist" Party. And many of the I.L.P leaders know it. But a name is not everything. And if in fact Labour does not by its active policy denote an exclusive class policy it can be regarded as immaterial what the actual Socialist and International party calls itself. It is now rather than later that the name is some disadvantage. Because the policy is still sufficiently incoherent for a name to be a cause of stumbling. I think most of our people accept the peace terms, mostly because they either do not know what they are or are too ill-instructed to know what they mean. The mass have been taught not to think during the war, or have found the problems so vast that they have given it up in despair. The terrible failure of the Liberal leaders is that they have been the direct agents of this obscuring of the political intellect and conscience of our people, instead of enlightening guides to a democratic policy. As a doubtful generalization I should say that the mass conscience of the upper and middle class had vanished altogether for the truce [?]. I have no doubt they accept the peace. But the better class worker I believe to be at least profoundly critical and discontented and widely furious at the Russian war. That rather than the bad peace is going to make the great revolutionary break in British opinion. Before very long organized Labour will set about reverting to a moral standard in politics. Till then and from other directions I fear all protesting will find little response. Have you read Trotsky's book on the Russian Revolution. Profoundly interesting! Also the articles by the American journalist coming out in the last week in the Herald are wonderfully enlightening.

DRO, 1148 M/792

FRANCIS ACLAND TO ELEANOR ACLAND

Late September 1919

I'm writing in the dark – literally – & particularly as to when you'll get this. I was due to leave yesterday afternoon – to cross last night but of course got stopped. Benn somehow got across from Liverpool. I expect he'd been at the Rusholme bye-election[1] & managed to get to a boat after the trains [?] stopped. We get no news of how the strike [2] is going & hear only of the trains – one up today – but no news of any going down. I don't know what to do about Ireland.

If I go now say on Tuesday or Wednesday I shall have to be away all the next week to get anything decent done, and I don't want to do that as it means missing ten days of the India Committee – which is rather too much. … I'm writing on the assumption that the strike will be short, but I can't really see how it can be. I feel sure that neither side left any solution unexplored before the strike was decided upon – & that therefore it must mean a real fight. If the Government succeed in keeping the towns fed it will be a marvel of organisation, but I think all the time of babies without milk. We shall be learning a bit of what we put the Germans through for months. I wish I really trusted Lloyd George and the Government more. Ll[oyd] G[eorge] is not above using the thing for election purposes.

[1.] The Rusholme by-election in Manchester on 7 October 1919 was significant since the Liberals had hoped to build on their by-election successes earlier in the year. In the event the party failed to improve on its general election result and the psychological victory went to Labour, which came a good second to the Conservatives.
[2.] Considerable disruption was caused in Britain at this time as a result of a major railway strike.

Cornish Post, 14/02/20

FRANCIS ACLAND TO JOHN TABB[1]

5, Barton Street, Westminster, 4 February 1920

My dear Mr Tabb.

You will remember that at a meeting of the Liberal delegates of the Camborne Parliamentary Division, held recently, I suggested that the best way of enabling the party to poll its utmost available strength at the next election might be to have a candidate in the field who could give full time to organising and educational work in the Division. In order to make this course possible, and to avoid any chance of my seeming to leaving the party in the lurch later on, I thought it right to let you know that reasons of health and the pressure of new and heavy responsibilities[2] which have come upon me in the West of England since the last election make it practically certain that I ought not to stand for the Division at the next election. Even now, as you know, these reasons, combined with heavy work in London make it impossible for me to be in the Division as much as I should like.

I need hardly say that the selection of another candidate will not affect my present work in and for the Division, or my obligations to the Liberal Association, which I shall continue to carry on to the best of my ability.

I think that perhaps my position should be known and therefore ask you to be kind enough to communicate this letter to the Press.

Yours most truly,

F.D. Acland

1. John Tabb, J.P., was the secretary of the Camborne Liberal Association.
2. Refers to the estate commitments of Francis following the death of Charles Acland on 18 February 1919.

DRO, 1148 M/1016

ELEANOR ACLAND TO RICHARD ACLAND

1920?

Daddy has been asked to stand as Liberal candidate for this part of the world[1] & he's going to. He's rather pleased, & I should think he'll get in. Of course we don't known when the Election will be – not yet awhile.

1. A reference to the selection of Francis as Liberal candidate for Tiverton. In the event he narrowly lost in 1922 by 74 votes but won with a majority of 403 in a by-election on 21 June 1923.

DRO, 1148 M/1018

ELEANOR ACLAND TO RICHARD ACLAND

Late May 1921

The North Ireland elections [1] have ended in the Unionists getting 40 seats, the Sinn Feiners only twelve. But it wasn't a fair election. We have put a lot of S[inn]. Feiners in prison & we would not allow them to vote. Also the country was being policed by special constables who are the old Carson rebels[2], so you can imagine it wasn't very safe for Sinn Feiners. Also we allowed no Sinn Fein meetings to be held, & we caught & put in prison their election agents. So I don't see that we can judge what Ulster thinks by the result of such unfair elections. Meanwhile there has been a terrific blaze in Dublin – a building worth a million burnt by S[inn].F[einer]s. I suppose this is tit for tat for the Black & Tans[3] burning the best buildings in Cork. We don't get much further by this endless tit-for-tat business. Nor do the Government seem to have any idea of settling the coal strike. Its very wonderful that a million miners have been idle for 8 weeks & yet no rioting or disorder; it just shows English working men are not mad Bolsheviks whatever people say against them.[4]

[1] A separate Parliament of Northern Ireland, which consisted of a House of Commons and a Senate, was created under the partition arrangements of the Government of Ireland Act 1920. The first elections were held on 24 May 1921 using a system of proportional representation. Although Eleanor lists the twelve non-Unionist MPs as all members of Sinn Fein, six of these MPs were actually Irish Nationalists.

[2] A reference to those pre-war Unionists under the leadership of Sir Edward Carson who had been prepared to resist self-government for Ireland.

[3] This was the phrase used to describe the British auxiliary police force sent to control Ireland in 1920. The brutality associated with the force alienated liberal public opinion in Britain. Many in the force were ex-servicemen and the nickname 'Black and Tans' arose from their black and khaki uniform.

[4] Industrial unrest in the immediate post-war period led Lloyd George to make a series of anti-Socialist speeches accusing the Labour movement of supporting Bolshevism.

DRO, 1148 M/1012

ELEANOR ACLAND TO RICHARD ACLAND

1921

This week I went up to London for 2 nights. The first night I spoke at a meeting in the street about Ireland, to a big crowd of poor people who listened hard. On the second night Daddy & I went to the King's Ball at Buckingham Palace, which was very grand indeed. All the men in uniform instead of ordinary black coats, & the women mostly wearing gorgeous jewels, & millions of lights blazing. The King & Queen of the Belgians were there; he looks a nice sensible man & she looks very clever & amusing. General Smuts[1] was there but I didn't catch sight of him. I saw Sir H. Craig[2], the Prime Minister of the Parliament at Belfast, & Lord Carson[3] who began the rebellion in Ireland against Home Rule & Sir Hamar Greenwood[4], the brute whom we have in charge of Ireland now. He was the only one of the three who looked really horrid – & so thoroughly pleased with himself. Everybody was talking about Ireland, & hoping that things are going to be settled. At any rate there is going to be a truce beginning Monday. Gen[eral] McReady[5] came out from his fortress in Dublin & drove through the streets to a meeting with the Sinn Feiners to settle about having a truce. The Dublin crowds could hardly believe their eyes to see him driving along in an open car with no guards, but as soon as they recognised him they greeted him with cheers. Which just shows how ready the "wicked" Irish are to make friends.

[1] Jan Christian Smuts (1870–1950) founded the South African Defence Force in the First World War and represented South Africa at the post-war Paris Peace Conference. He served as Prime Minister of South Africa from 1919–23 and again from 1939–48.

[2] Sir James Craig (1871–1940) served in the Boer War and was elected to the House of Commons as a Unionist MP in 1906. He became Viscount Craigavon in 1927 and served as the first Prime Minister of Northern Ireland from June 1921 until his death.

[3] Sir Edward Henry Carson (1854–1935) was Unionist MP for Dublin University 1892–1918 and Belfast Duncairn 1918–21. He was the pre-war leader of the Irish Unionists, Attorney General 1915, First Lord of the Admiralty 1916–17 and Minister without Portfolio 1917–18. He became Lord Carson in 1921.

[4] Sir Thomas Hamar Greenwood (1870–1948) was the Liberal (and then Coalition Liberal) MP for York 1906–10 and Sunderland December 1910–22. Served as Secretary for Overseas Trade 1919–20 and Chief Secretary for Ireland 1920–22. He was Constitutionalist (and then Conservative) MP for Walthamstow East 1924–29 and went to the House of Lords as Lord Greenwood in 1929.

[5] Presumably General Sir Cecil Frederick Macready (1862–1946) who served in Africa 1899–1902 and with the British Expeditionary Force in France 1914–16. He was Commissioner of the Metropolitan Police 1918–20 and Commander in Chief in Ireland 1920–22.

Spectator, 04/06/21.

ELEANOR ACLAND TO THE EDITOR OF THE 'SPECTATOR'

Sprydoncote, Exeter, June 1921

Sir,

In your issue of May 21ˢᵗ an anonymous correspondent calling himself "Southern Irishman" refers to a recent article in the *Westminster Gazette*, written by a lady, containing an interview with the Chairman of the Kerry County Council. The only article which has recently appeared in the *Westminster* even remotely resembling "Southern Irishman's" description was one which I contributed[1] on April 29ᵗʰ. I am interested in your correspondent's description of that article, because it enables me to judge what sort of travesty of Irish affairs is contained in the rest of the letter. There was not a word in my article of "soft, pathetic eyes"; nor did I retail any tall talk uttered by the Chairman of the Kerry County Council. I remember one fact only which he mentioned against the British authorities – namely that the commandant of the Cadet Corps at Tralee had commandeered thirty bedsteads from Tralee Workhouse, leaving the inmates to sleep on straw mattresses on the floor. This at the time I myself pooh-poohed till I had verified it myself by a visit to the workhouse. I did think it rather odd that after a whole month had elapsed since this particular contingent of ex-officers had arrived the British Government had not been able to afford bedsteads for them, but had had to rob the paupers. I daresay the beds have since been returned. I hope so. Nor was it tall or short talk, but actual fact, that my second interview with the Chairman of the County Council took place in Tralee gaol, where he had been locked up without charge or trial by the military authorities, just as 2,500 other Irishmen have been locked up. He is still in gaol, neither charged with nor tried for any offence. Your correspondent is mistaken in one point, among others. We do not abuse England; this Government is by no means the whole of England. There is also the England which, luckily for the Empire, gave South Africa self-government in 1906.

I am,

Sir, &c.,

Eleanor Acland, J.P.

---

[1] Eleanor had been sent to Ireland by the Women's National Liberal Federation to make a first-hand report on the Irish civil war. It was claimed that her report was a factor in the loss of support for the government's Irish policy. See *The Liberal Women's News,* November 1925, pp. 109–10.

DRO, 1148 M/1023

ELEANOR ACLAND TO RICHARD ACLAND

June 1921?

I'm horribly busy – having been in London two days or three, so letters have settled upon my table like drifts of snow. And tomorrow we have the big Liberal party at Killerton[1] – 1000 people coming. Ellen[2] & I have been tying 3lbs of sweets into 1d bundles. . . . There was a letter of mine in the Spectator. I had a meeting in London about Ireland, & it was a good one. Things seem to be as bad as ever, only that more English people are getting angry. Reprisals are going on – Ll[oyd]. George can't stop his own men now.

[1] In the 1920s Killerton was described as 'The Castle Beautiful of Liberalism' as a result of the regular meetings held in the grounds for party supporters.

[2] Ellen Acland (1913–24) was the only daughter of Eleanor and Francis. She died tragically as a result of a cycling accident on the Killerton estate.

DM 668, National Liberal Club collection of election addresses

FRANCIS ACLAND TO THE ELECTORS OF THE TIVERTON DIVISION

Killerton, 21 November 1923

Dear Sir or Madam,

I appeal to you with the greatest confidence to send me back to Parliament once more as your member. I have, as yet, had only seven weeks of Parliamentary life as member for the Tiverton Division.[1]

The Government which promised us five years of tranquillity has within a year plunged us into an entirely unnecessary election. They do it because Mr. Baldwin thinks that unemployment can be stopped only by putting duties on imported goods. They offer no proof and take care that we shall be so rushed that we shall have no time to think it out. They won't tell us how high the duties will be or what they will be put upon. It is to be verdict first, trial afterwards. Everything may be taxed except wheat, meat, bacon, cheese, butter and eggs.

I tell you straight that I don't like and don't want any extra taxes. I want less taxes, not more, and I don't believe that employment can be increased by any system of taxation.

As a matter of fact you will find that our present unemployment is not such as can be cured by taxing imports. Nine-tenths of our unemployment is either in trades not affected by imports, or in trades in which there are less imports than before the war, when there was practically no unemployment, and that shows that it is not the imports which cause the distress. I find that four of the worst trades for unemployment are Building, Engineering, Ship-Building, and Coal Mining. How will taxes on imports stop them? It will just put up the cost of living, and so prevent men and women from buying so much, and that will make unemployment worse.

They say that France and other countries with Protection have no unemployment. This may be true, but France is keeping under arms more men than we have unemployed, and paying them with the money which ought to be repaid to us, and France has only half the people for each square mile that we have. It would be easy enough to give everyone work if our population was down to that of Protectionist countries. But our great population has been built up on Free Trade, and no one can give them more work by artificial restrictions on that trade.

A cure for unemployment will only come when some other government takes up the task, which Mr. Baldwin has abandoned, of restoring the economic position of Europe, and of increasing our reliance on the League of Nations.

I turn from the national position to consider the position of the constituency for which on this day five months ago I was given an honourable responsibility. I say without fear of contradiction that no trade, occupation or profession carried on in the Tiverton Division can show even a reasonable probability of benefiting from Mr. Baldwin's proposals. Let us look first at Agriculture. Farmers have had bounties given them once, and they were swept away by the strongest Government we have ever had, after only six months' trial. Mr. Baldwin promises them again, but what does he say: *"Neither agriculture nor any other industry in this country can look to this government, nor any other government, whatever promise they may make, for a direct or indirect subsidy of public money."* Our farmers are not fools, and they know that if they are had once it is the Government's fault, but if they are had twice it will be their own fault.

In any case on most of our farms the extra money the farmers may have to pay for fertilisers, feeding stuffs, implements and machinery, binder twine, saddlery, and their own and their families' boots and clothes and household requirements will more than use up anything they may get from the bounty, and leave no margin for extra wages. Then when the bounty is swept away, as it was before, there's still the extra to pay, and nothing coming back!

I am very keen on establishing a policy for Agriculture which will stand firm in spite of changes of government, and give the industry real stability and security, and I believe it can be done; but to trust to Mr. Baldwin's bounties is simply to build on sand.

What are the occupations of the rest of our people, and how will they be able to make good the extra cost of the articles taxed? Remember that everything except the six articles of food may be taxed: clothes, boots, household requirements, tools, furniture, everything.

We have agricultural workers who were had before over the Wages Boards, and will not be likely to trust the Government again.

We have quarrymen, who have no foreign competition against which they can be protected, makers of silk and woollen goods who have only to ask their employers in order to be told that the change would make things worse and not better, paper-makers who will find it difficult to get a tax put on paper as long as the newspapers demand free imports.

We have ministers of religion, doctors, solicitors and other professional men; we have shop-keepers, hotel-keepers, inn-keepers and lodging-house keepers, who will not be able to increase their charges.

We have clerks, accountants, agents and travellers, who will get no higher salaries, and people employed by Government or Local Authorities such as soldiers and sailors, teachers and police, County Hospital attendants, and postmen, roadmen and rate collectors who will not find it at all easy to get higher pay. We have railway-men in the same position, and many retired officers from all our public services, all on fixed incomes.

We have fishermen, and no tariff will make more salmon run up the Exe.

We have a great many old people, and particularly old-age pensioners, living on limited means, who could very ill afford to pay higher prices for the things they buy.

These are the people whom I am out to look after. None of them are doing too well, and I will strive with all my strength to prevent the cost of living for any of them from being increased.

Many of them are by nature Conservative, but many Conservatives like Sir Robert Newman[2] will think it right to stand and vote for Free Trade in this election, in which it is the only issue.

I appeal, therefore, to all of them most confidently for support.

The Tiverton Division has always hitherto re-elected its sitting member, and I trust you may consider me worthy of the same confidence which you have shown to your members in former years. If you do, I do not think I shall let you down.

I remain,
Yours truly and faithfully,
Francis D. Acland

1. Earlier that year Francis had returned to the House of Commons following his victory in the Tiverton by-election on 21 June 1923.
2. Sir Robert Hunt Stapylton Dudley Lydston Newman (1871–1945) was Conservative (later Independent) MP for the neighbouring seat of Exeter 1918–31. His maverick stance on a variety of issues, including free trade, meant that the local Conservative association adopted a new candidate in 1927. Newman had the party whip withdrawn from him but retained his seat as an Independent in 1929. He became Baron Mamhead in 1931.

DM 668, National Liberal Club collection of election addresses

FRANCIS ACLAND TO THE ELECTORS OF THE TIVERTON DIVISION

Killerton, 20 October 1924

Ladies and Gentlemen,

For the fourth time in less than two years I have the honour of asking you to support me with your votes. The electors of the Tiverton Division have never yet turned against the man whom they have elected. Why should they now? If you will only judge me by what I have done before and since the last election I have no fear of the result.

I had no share in putting the Government in for after the Conservatives' inevitable defeat, the new Government were quite constitutionally called to office, without any vote by the House of Commons. I have, however, as a Member of Parliament supported their Budget and the extension of Old Age Pensions, and the Housing Act, and the setting up of Agricultural Wages Committees, and have backed up in every way the work of strengthening the League of Nations and bringing greater security and peace to Europe. I did this because I believed, with Mr Baldwin, that a Labour Government should be given every chance of making good.

Three things in particular I have had the good fortune to be able to do personally:-

1. As Chairman of the Liberal Agricultural members in the House of Commons I worked out a way of improving the Wages Board Bill, which resulted in the compromise which placed it on the Statute Book.[1] But for this it would not be law now, and, as you know, both sides in the industry are now preparing to work the Act in a friendly way. This was my doing.

2. After 21 years of effort I have brought the movement for the co-operative

organisation of agriculture to the point when the National Farmers Union have taken it over as a going concern and their leaders have expressed gratitude to me for my work on behalf of the farming industry.

3. I have helped to work and press forward schemes for the expansion of forestry which will be set going this winter, and give a great deal of fresh employment.

You will find in a speech by me, of which a copy is enclosed, the causes of the present General Election. I think the Liberals were right in asking for an enquiry[2], but Mr Ramsay MacDonald has preferred an inquest, and I believe the country's verdict will be "unjustifiable self-destruction". There ought not, however, to be such frequent elections, and I should vote for having at least three years between elections, so long as any party can be found able and willing to carry on the government of the country.

That speech also contains the main outlines of a new policy for making the best use of the land and giving full security to good cultivators. We cannot cure industrial unrest by merely denouncing Socialism. There must be some positive remedy, and I put forward my policy, which I have been thinking out for years, not as a party policy but as one which all can support.

It is a good Labour policy, because it gives the worker a better chance of making a good living on the land.

It is a good Liberal policy, as it frees the land for the best use.

It is a good Conservative policy, as it aims at settling people securely on the land as the true basis of national safety.

If you think the proposals good you will, I believe, vote for the man who can help to put them through.

In town and country alike I believe that much can be done to help men to become the owners of their houses or business premises, and I will work for this until it is done.

I have worked hard for Service and Ex-Servicemen regardless of party politics, and have got a good many things put right. I will do so again if returned.

I will never vote for any class against other classes, but always for all, and I believe that my twenty year's experience of national work helps me to find ways of keeping people together in a friendly way while always pressing forward to better things. I am no Conservative, and never shall be. Vague promises, but little done, are not in my line, but hard work for the people. I am no Socialist, and never shall be. How could I, brought up to value individual liberty, favour a barren policy of taking over all our agriculture and industries and putting them under centralized and sterilizing official control?

If we are to have safety and quiet and progress, the Liberal Party, must be given a chance of Government. There will be no real peace under the

Conservatives, who are pledged to Protection, which the country does not want. Nor will there be real peace with Labour the masters of the country, for they are pledged to nationalize all production and trade, and the country does not want that.

Safety at this time lies in a strong, progressive middle party. To build houses, to find employment, to develop the land, – that will be our task – whilst we press forward steadily, through arbitration agreements and disarmament, to the time when war shall be no more.

Will you not trust me to go on with this work? I think you will.

Yours very truly and faithfully.

Francis D. Acland

---

1. For a brief consideration of the position of Francis in relation to the bill see Ian Packer, *Lloyd George, Liberalism and the Land: The Land Issue and Party Politics in England, 1906–1914*, Royal Historical Society, 2001, pp. 185–86.
2. The Liberal party had proposed the establishment of a Select Committee to inquire into the handling of the Campbell case. MacDonald had apparently preferred an early dissolution to a compromise agreement and the Labour government's defeat in the Commons led to the general election.

DRO, 1148 M/1030

ELEANOR ACLAND TO RICHARD ACLAND

Knightshayes Court, Tiverton, 31 October 1924

Dearest Dick,

... You will, like us, be shocked & sad at our own defeat & the defeat of nearly all Daddy's friends. The only thing to be said is that its such a violent swing that there must be a swing back soon, but will it be a swing right over to Socialism? I am ever so glad you came down. Don't think it wasn't worthwhile. You have made heaps of friends in both camps – & perhaps paved the way to yourself being member here some ten or fifteen years hence – Liberal member perhaps, or called by some other name but meaning much the same thing.

The Labour Party have done a lot of harm. They would have it we, the Lib[eral]s, were going too slow, but they didn't know what we were up against. Now they've tried to risk things & instead of using the chance we gave them to govern wisely they have got stampeded by their wild men. Result – a counter stampede to reaction. Next result? Lord knows!

Gilbert & Gladys[1] were very nice about it all & so far we have not heard of any rows or nonsense.
Your loving Mummy.

[1] Lieutenant-Colonel Sir Gilbert John Acland-Troyte (1876–1964) and his wife Gladys. Acland-Troyte contested Tiverton in both the by-election and general election of 1923. He was related to Francis and was Conservative MP for Tiverton 1924–45.

DRO, 1148 M/1031

ELEANOR ACLAND TO RICHARD ACLAND

Killerton, Exeter, 9 November 1924

Armistice Sunday again, & here we have Birkenhead[1] & Churchill in the cabinet again, who believe in the glory of war as wildly as ever any old-fashioned Hun ever did. Protection, too, in various guises, due to come along, & the whole theory of Protection is based on feelings that make for hatred & jealousy between peoples. Well, I don't think its satisfactory, in fact its pretty black. Daddy feels rather despairing about the Liberal party's revival, but all the Lib[eral]s in the villages here are in great heart. I go to London tomorrow & there's a big reception to hear Asquith speak in the evening. Perhaps he'll cheer up Daddy.

[1] Sir F.E. Smith (1872–1930) was Secretary of State for India 1924–28 in Baldwin's Conservative government. He had previously served as Attorney General 1916–19 and Lord Chancellor 1919–22. Created Baron Birkenhead in 1919 and Earl of Birkenhead in 1922.

DRO, 1148 M/1032

ELEANOR ACLAND TO RICHARD ACLAND

Killerton, Exeter, 16 November 1924

Have you seen anything of Dingle Foot?[1] He seems to be a remarkably clever man, & if he's anything like his father ought to turn into a great man. We had a most enthusiastic meeting at Dawlish last night, & quite a procession of little girls came up with bunches of flowers for me. The young people are very keen that you should take the lead in a League of Young Liberals. Yesterday our new parson was instituted. I enclose the service. The church was packed & so it will be today I expect for the first sermon. He has a splendid voice & Daddy & I feel him already to be a real friend.

> Your v[ery] loving,
> Mother

[1.] Sir Dingle Mackintosh Foot (1905–78) was the eldest son of Isaac Foot. He succeeded Francis as the Liberal candidate for Tiverton and came second in 1929. Liberal MP for Dundee 1931–45 and parliamentary secretary at the Ministry of Economic Warfare 1940–45. After defecting to Labour in 1956 he became MP for Ipswich 1957–70 and Solicitor General 1964–67.

DRO, 1148 M/1033

ELEANOR ACLAND TO RICHARD ACLAND

Killerton, Exeter, 20 November 1924

League of Young Liberals. Great keenness is working up about this. Mr Isaac Foot says his son can come & give us a start here, & you in return must give them a [talk?] in his division. It is proposed to collect bands of Y[oung]. L[iberals] at Tiverton for a afternoon in January. It must be about 8th or 9th or 10th. Could you see Dingle Foot & ask him for either of these dates? He could stay here. As soon as you know please write & tell Arnold Riley Esq, Dawlish, Devon. He is the leader of the movement here & is getting up this gathering. If you can't get Dingle, tell him so, & tell him that you yourself will come. We had a grand meeting last night with Mr Foot as chief speaker.

DRO, 1148 M/1048

ELEANOR ACLAND TO RICHARD ACLAND

Killerton, Exeter, 1 February 1925

Dearest Dick,

I wish I had made an effort to get you up to London for the Albert Hall Liberal meeting . . . Perhaps you couldn't have come. But if you could it would have given you a new idea of the Liberal party. I suppose you may have read about it, but that's not the same thing. We really did get the feeling of being in a big army, that meant business & that nothing could stop. Of course coming away into the outside world was rather a drop, still there are memories which I hope will remain really powerful. About the most moving thing in the whole meeting was the speech of a young man called Kingsley Griffith[1] representing the L[eague of] Y[oung] L[iberals]. He was a candidate at the last election, but he only looked about twenty three. His speech was so very plain & courageous that all the 10,000 people in the hall just went on cheering for about five minutes . . .

I think it's a very good sign that the Liberals are so pleased about young people coming back to them & it also shows of course how very sad it's been that the keenest young people have been going away. We had two days convention & then the big Albert Hall meeting. The convention began in rather a muddled way & it had too much to discuss. All through the greatest enthusiasm was shown for working-men & women, young Liberals, and any speech which showed dash & courage. I feel thoroughly encouraged by it all.

[1.] Frank Kingsley Griffith (1889–1962) contested Bromley as a Liberal in 1922, 1923 and 1924. He was Liberal MP for Middlesbrough West 1928–40. Served as Parliamentary Private Secretary to Herbert Samuel at the Home Office 1931–32 and resigned from the House of Commons in 1940 when he was appointed as a County Court Judge.

DRO, 1148 M/1070

ELEANOR ACLAND TO RICHARD ACLAND

Killerton, Exeter, Autumn 1925?

Look in the Nov[ember]: Contemporary Review (2/6) for Daddy's article on the Land Policy. It seems to me the best thing on it yet published. I am going to Wales on Monday to speak on that matter at Cardiff, Abergavenny, Monmouth, etc. Dear old Gilbert[1] has pronounced on the whole scheme "Absurd!" So typically Tory to dismiss a new idea founded on years of thought as Absurd simply because it is new . . .

I've been off in London one day this week, trying to get Lib[eral] women to plump for the Land Policy. Some of the C[ommit]tee are keen but some are the opposite.

[1] Refers to Gilbert Acland-Troyte who was mentioned earlier.

_____

DRO, 1148 M/1066

ELEANOR ACLAND TO RICHARD ACLAND

Killerton, Exeter, Autumn 1925?

We are in for a fearful tussle over Ll[oyd] G[eorge]'s Land Policy. Some of our local mug-wumps are very anti. Thorne[1] wrote to Daddy & suggested that nothing more should be said about it in public till after the N[ational]. L[iberal]. F[ederation]. conference.[2] To which Daddy replied: Very well, but if the Exec[utive] decides so that will mean that neither I nor Mrs Acland nor Richard can speak in the Division. He then took Thorne to two meetings & spoke about nothing else, & Thorne was rather surprised (he admitted) at the enthusiasm evoked. There is a terrible timidity about the Liberal party big-wigs, specially the Little big-wigs, which we must somehow knock out before we can become a winning party.

[1] William Thorne was the treasurer of the Tiverton Liberal Association at this time.
[2] Critics of Lloyd George's land policy claimed that it had been produced by a private committee and before any further discussion it had to be agreed by a special conference of the National Liberal Federation, which eventually met on 17–19 February 1926. On 13 November 1925 the executive committee of the Tiverton Liberal Association passed a resolution that effectively prevented Francis from speaking in favour of the policy at meetings in the constituency.

_____

DRO, 1148 M/1069

ELEANOR ACLAND TO RICHARD ACLAND

Killerton, Exeter, 25 November 1925

I hope Daddy got on well at the Cambridge Union[1] – of course haven't had time to hear yet. I feel thoroughly worried about the Liberal party – the leaders are just awful! Runciman[2] attacking the Land Policy as if he were a Tory. I mean not trying to see the good in it, but deliberately misrepresenting things. e.g. saying "Farmers are to be run by committees." Well, well, your generation may see better days, & anyhow all parties seem to be suffering from the same disease. So we must peg away.

Your Loving Mummy.

[1.] In November 1925 Francis was the chief speaker at the Cambridge Union on a motion in favour of the Land Policy.

[2.] Walter Runciman (see above) had emerged as a leading opponent of Lloyd George after the 1924 election. Although essentially a libertarian in regard to party policy, he led the so-called Radical Group of Liberal MPs, including leading left-wingers like Benn and Kenworthy, which was opposed to Lloyd George's chairmanship of the parliamentary party.

DRO, 1148 M/1076

ELEANOR ACLAND TO RICHARD ACLAND

Killerton, Exeter, 31 January 1926

The only other thing that has happened is that I went & made a Liberal speech at Bath which so impressed myself that I reversed my previous decision which was that politics are a rotten game & I'd have no more to do with them. I now think that if you believe in your party's principles at all you are most of all bound to work for them when the party is in difficulties.

I am very glad you are hearing some of the Labour people. I don't wonder they are angry, all the same I don't think society can be amended by working from the point of view of one class. It is tempting to think: "The rich have been top-dogs for too long: now if we can only down them we shall have our turn at top-dogging. And then everything will be all right".

I travelled with some miners on the way from Bath – all very angry & desperate & sure that if only royalties were done away with there would be heaps of money for better wages. Of course seeing the problems of luxury etc in the papers they think there is somewhere a big surplus of money which could go to wages. Whereas there is not, & wages can only increase if production goes up, & production will only go up when owners & workers both agree as to what shares each shall have.

I think a coal subsidy[1] might be good if arranged like this:

A subsidy to be paid to each mine, but <u>only</u> on each ton of coal produced above the average amount produced in the mine during the corresponding month of the last three or two years: & only on condition that half the Subsidy goes to the miners, half to the owners. This would cause the worst paying almost out-worked mines to shut up, & attract workers & enterprise to the mines which could hope to increase their output.

There is no Tiverton candidate yet, but as the Amorys definitely wouldn't support you I don't suppose the rest of the Executive would invite you.[2]

Talking of, & going back to, miners – a Liberal in Tiverton told me his brother was boss of all the overground work connected with a certain big mine in Derbyshire (I think) & his wage was £2.10.0 in a good week, and his rent 17/0, so that brings him, the boss, almost down to the level of the agric[ultural] labourer. He told me that he (the speaker) & his wife on an income of £3 a week after felt so sorry for the brother's children that they pinched themselves & send him a few shillings. "And mind you", he said, "if that's what my brother gets what about them that are at the bottom of the ladder?"

I don't know what we can do. If we were really in earnest I suppose we'd renounce all luxury & social swank & live like the poor, & spend all we could save on cottages. But life pulls in so many directions.

Your loving <u>Mummy</u>

[1] The idea behind a coal subsidy was that the state should subsidise the coal industry to enable employers to maintain wages while not increasing prices. A subsidy had been introduced in July 1925 but the government's refusal to renew the scheme when it expired on 30 April 1926 was the catalyst for the announcement of wage cuts and the onset of the General Strike in May 1926.

[2] On 18 December 1925 Francis finally confirmed that he was standing down as Liberal prospective candidate for Tiverton. Opposition to his stance on land reform was led by Sir Ian Amory, the president of the Tiverton Liberal Association. Amory was not even prepared to accept the modified programme agreed in February 1926 and he eventually defected to the Conservatives.

DRO, 1148 M/1073

ELEANOR ACLAND TO RICHARD ACLAND

Killerton, Exeter, 7 February 1926

Your thing for the Pioneers[1] was good – it will have to go in March. I think you might revise it & eliminate some of the 'I's for the sake of style. Perhaps that sounds trivial. But style [is] very important because in some odd way the effect on people who read depends on it. Bergson says that in writing you have to make people's minds dance, & get the same tune going in their minds as in your own. Your point about miners not considering agric[ultural] labourers is very good I think. It is the selfishness & rather narrowness of the Labour people that makes them inadequate. Of course we can't blame them for selfishness, it is only the response to selfishness that they have been up against. Still if you are going to settle a problem you must have the sense of all the sides to it.

I hear Mr Lloyd George was going to ask you to go to the conference & to lunch with him. I hope that has come off. Ll[oyd] G[eorge] is being violently abused in letters to the Nation – raking up all his past blunders. People who feel they can't stick to the Liberal party because he is one of their leaders ought to have walked out last year. This useless bickering simply disheartens everyone. Ll[oyd] G[eorge] himself is behaving with extraordinary magnanimity it seems to me.[2]

[1.] Presumably a reference to the magazine of the Tiverton Liberal Association.
[2.] Trevor Wilson in *The Downfall of the Liberal Party 1914–1935*, London, 1966, claims that Lloyd George's conciliatory approach during the period from December 1925–February 1926 enabled him to win over the support of former opponents in groups like the Liberal and Radical Candidates Association. This new support was critical at the time of his final showdown with Asquith later that year (pp. 327–28).

DRO, 1148 M/1024

ELEANOR ACLAND TO RICHARD ACLAND

Killerton, Exeter, 14 February 1926

I am glad Ll[oyd] G[eorge] had a successful visit to Oxford. The other Liberal leaders don't seem able to forgive him his popularity. They are very jealous, I suppose because none of them are anything like so popular. I think because none of them seem so keen to be enjoying politics so much, they're all so dreadfully high brow & serious & self important and in a word priggish over it.

We had a meeting of Liberal delegates in Exeter on Friday. It was rather dismal – so obvious that Ian Amory & Francis are on quite opposite tacks now. Many of the delegates spoke up well for the Ll[oyd] G[eorge] Land Policy & showed considerable resentment at the way the Exec[utive] C[ommit]tee had shelved Francis. They had a rather fruitless discussion as to how our 3 delegates should vote at the Land Conference.

Sir Ian proposed that they should vote against anything which made it more difficult for a good man to obtain <u>ownership</u> of his farm. But nobody seconded. Two of the delegates – Farmer Lake & Cursons who is a small holder risen to a farmer & <u>ought</u> to have simply said they hadn't considered the matter much. The third, Leach, a small-holder was more coherent.[1]

But there! The whole thing is so incoherent now. Ll[oyd] G[eorge] still talks as if the modified programme was the basis of a real change, but I don't see it. I wish he hadn't felt obliged to modify.[2] He did it of course out of loyalty to the party, to avoid a split, but small thanks he has got for it! The anti-Green Book people still talk & work as if no modification had been made.

[1.] On 12 February 1926 a special meeting of Tiverton Liberal Association in Exeter appointed V.G. Leach, S. Cursons and William Lake, a vice-president of the association, as its three delegates to the Land Conference. The meeting suggested that Francis was still popular with the wider membership of the association. See Devon Record Office, Tiverton Liberal Association papers, 4996G/A1, special meeting, 12 February 1926.

[2.] In February 1926 Lloyd George agreed to a significant compromise over the controversial policy of 'cultivating tenure'. This aspect of the Land Policy had been especially criticised by his opponents as 'land nationalisation'. See Wilson, *Downfall of the Liberal Party*, p. 327.

DRO, 1148 M/1086

ELEANOR ACLAND TO RICHARD ACLAND

Killerton, Exeter, 23 May 1926

Dearest Dick,

Well, the 'situation' doesn't clear up does it? I wonder how soon, if ever, the public will wake up to the fact that Baldwin, for all his good-nature & honesty, has no real grasp of the job. If he'd taken a strong line & been more energetic a year ago, the strike need never have come at all.[1] But now no one seems to take in anything more than the fact that, given the strike, he managed to get it stopped. It's deplorable that Liberal quarrels should have started up again. Personally I think Ll[oyd] G[eorge]. was right in showing more sympathy with the strikes than the other Liberal leaders did.[2] The strike order itself may have been a mistake, even a wicked mistake. But the reason it got obeyed was not that Trade Unionists are revolutionary, but that there existed in the average working-man's mind a strong feeling that the miners were being "done down" & a real desire to strike a blow on their behalf.

I'm afraid there is no Liberal party, in the real sense of the word – no organised body of people who think alike. We are too much just a collection of people who haven't quite made up our minds what we think. If a new party emerges, led by Ll[oyd] G[eorge] & the more reasonable Labour men, I would rather belong to that.

[1] Baldwin's refusal to renew the Coal subsidy in the previous month had led to the miners being locked out by their employers who wanted longer hours and lower wages. A General Strike was called by the TUC on 3 May 1926 in support of the miners but the government used troops, special constables and volunteers to maintain essential services and the strike ended after just nine days. The demoralised miners were eventually forced back to work in November 1926.

[2] Differing reactions to the General Strike resulted in a final confrontation between Asquith and Lloyd George. While the Liberal Shadow Cabinet sided with Baldwin against the strikers, Lloyd George called for moderation and claimed that the government should also be criticised for its handling of events.

DRO, 1148 M/1087

ELEANOR ACLAND TO RICHARD ACLAND

Killerton, Exeter, 30 May 1926

I hear from Miss Harvey that you are to be asked to speak at the Women's Liberal Council on Tuesday June 22. But they only want quite a short speech. I wonder if you will go. Personally I feel on the edge of saying: "I will not stir another finger for the Liberal party as long as the machinery of the party is in the hands of a small coterie whose main idea of Liberal work is to jockey Ll[oyd] G[eorge]. out of the party.[1] "As far as I can see there is no real reason of policy or principle for this latest row. Ll[oyd] G[eorge] had laid more stress than the other Liberal leaders on a certain aspect of the [national?] trouble – namely that it was the Government's fault. But I'm quite sure the rank & file agree with him in that, specially the young & go-ahead. Had I been a Hammersmith Liberal I would have voted Labour I know, as a protest ag[ain]st the way that the Libe[eral] party is run; though I daresay that would have been a silly thing to do, I'm sure quite a lot of Hammersmith Liberals did it.[2]

[1.] A reference to the campaign against Lloyd George in May 1926 by Asquith's supporters in the Shadow Cabinet.
[2.] The Hammersmith by-election on 28 May 1926 resulted in a Labour gain from the Conservatives. In comparison with 1923 the Liberal share of the vote fell from 22.2 to 8.0 per cent and this was seen as the critical factor in the Labour victory.

DRO, 1148 M/1088

ELEANOR ACLAND TO RICHARD ACLAND

Falcon Hotel, Bude, 3 June 1926

As to what Aubrey Herbert[1] says about Ll[oyd] G[eorge] the mere fact that Francis has never had a penny from him (not even to cover heavy expenses while attending the Land C[ommit]tee) just shows how inaccurate & biased his "information" is. But that remark of his "all Liberals hate Ll[oyd] G[eorge] except those who are in his pay" is just the sort of lie which Vivian[2] Pringle[3] & Co do disseminate (quite honestly perhaps they believe it). One would say such a lie is unforgivable, & the proof of Ll[oyd] G[eorge]'s genuine desire to save the Lib[eral] party is that he has so long gone on forgiving this & similar lies; even going so far as to water down his splendid Land Policy in order to secure unity. And has one of the opposite faction met him in any way? Have they gone about the country doing propaganda work for the agreed Land Policy? Not a word from one of them! And then they grouse because Ll[oyd] G[eorge] hasn't handed over his fund.

Daddy is going to stay the weekend with Lloyd George at his house in Surrey, together with Maynard Keynes[4] & Ramsay Muir[5] (two other unpaid supporters!). I was asked too but can't go. I suppose they are going to discuss a programme for a new party.

As to safeguarding[6] – I suppose if the system could be applied by a C[ommit]tee of men who possessed archangelic & a compatibility to an industrial life run entirely for the common good, it might & would be useful. But human nature being what it is you can't get over what a big Tory manufacturer said: "If Protection comes in it would pay me to spend £20,000 a year (which I now devote to keeping my plant up to date) on lobbying & bribing politicians". Also whatever system of Protection grows up in England, it's long certain to injure the rural part of the country. The overwhelming majority of town voters will never stand food taxes. Therefore everything will be taxed before farm produce, the country will be more & more drained of its population, & England will become even more than now badly balanced between unhealthy town & healthy country life.

Cubby & I are very happy here in a lazy way. Cubby keeps a wonderful aquarium – the creatures die a good deal but so they might on the shore.

Your loving mummy.

[1.] Possibly Aubrey Herbert who was Liberal candidate for the City of Chester in 1929 and 1931.

[2.] Vivian Phillipps (1870–1955) was one of the leading Liberals opposed to Lloyd George. He was Liberal MP for West Edinburgh 1922–24 and Chief Whip 1923–24. As Chairman of the Liberal Organisation Committee he was often linked to internal disagreements and in 1927 was forced out of office following the decision to accept support from Lloyd George's political fund.

[3.] William Mather Rutherford Pringle (1874–1928) was Liberal MP for North-West Lanarkshire 1910– 18 and Penistone 1922–24. He was regarded as one of Lloyd George's main opponents in the Liberal party and was the chairman of the Liberal and Radical Candidates Association.

[4.] John Maynard Keynes (1883–1946) was an influential economist whose radical ideas on using deficit spending to stimulate economic activity was central to Lloyd George's policy review in the late 1920s. He was a government advisor on war finance and reconstruction during the First World War and a leading figure in the Liberal Summer School movement. Created Baron Keynes in 1942.

[5.] Ramsay Muir (1872–1941) was a leading intellectual in the Liberal party. He was MP for Rochdale 1923–24 and as a co-founder of the Liberal Summer School in 1921 influenced the subsequent development of party policy. Muir was chairman of the National Liberal Federation 1931–33 and then president 1933–36.

[6.] Safeguarding was a protectionist scheme that had initially been introduced by the post-war Lloyd George coalition. It was then continued by Baldwin's 1924–29 administration whereby certain British industries such as lace and fabric gloves could obtain protective tariffs if they could demonstrate that they were suffering from unfair foreign competition.

DRO, 1148 M/1089

ELEANOR ACLAND TO RICHARD ACLAND

Bude, 6 June 1926

I wonder what Daddy, Ll[oyd] George & Co are talking about. I see the Liberal MPs asked for re-re-union[1], & sent Runciman, [Godfrey] Collins[2] & V[ivian]. Phillips to tell Asquith as much. Runciman who on that same evening declared that it was impossible to work in a cabinet containing Ll[oyd] G[eorge]! What is one to make of it?

Yours with love,

Mummy

[1.] The majority of those Liberal MPs who had survived the 1924 election tended to support Lloyd George. Their concern over the confrontational approach of Asquith and his supporters led to renewed calls for party unity.

[2.] Sir Godfrey Collins (see above) was Chief Whip of the Liberal party 1924–26

DRO, 1148 M/1090

ELEANOR ACLAND TO RICHARD ACLAND

Bude, 14 June 1926

Dearest Dick,

There may be a letter from you by second post. I don't seem to have had anything from you since a letter about a fortnight ago, saying what Aubrey Herbert said about Ll[oyd] George, etc, etc. You may like to see the letter of Daddy's about the Liberal Candidates meeting.[1] I presume the part about Violet Bonham Carter [2] is not a subject to be publicly mentioned, or even repeated in private talk.

The worst of it is I am afraid that the anti-Ll[oyd] G[eorge]. people will go on saying "Oh yes, Snowden denied the overtures & doubtless it was made worthwhile to him to do so – but no smoke without fire etc". And then how are we to know that they won't immediately start hatching up some other scandal? Well, one can only hope they've learnt a lesson this time.[3]

[1.] This meeting of the Liberal and Radical Candidates Association had discussed the claim that Lloyd George had met senior members of the Labour party at Snowden's home in May 1926 with the intention of defecting to Labour. However, Lloyd George was able to dismiss the claims of his opponents led by Pringle by producing a letter from Snowden that confirmed such a meeting did not take place. See Wilson, *Downfall of the Liberal Party*, p. 333.

2. Violet Bonham Carter (1887–1969) was the daughter of Herbert Asquith and his first wife Helen Melland. She was an energetic campaigner for her father in the 1920s and served as president of the Women's Liberal Federation 1923–25 and 1939–45. In 1964 she received a life peerage as Baroness Asquith.

3. In retrospect this incident actually marked a turning point in the confrontation between Asquith and Lloyd George. The Candidates Association expressed its confidence in Lloyd George and its call for unity was endorsed by the annual conference of the National Liberal Federation at Weston-super-Mare on 17–18 June. Asquith's position had been further undermined on 12 June when he suffered a stroke and on 15 October he announced his resignation as leader of the Liberal party.

Bristol, DM 668, National Liberal Club collection of election addresses

FRANCIS ACLAND TO THE ELECTORS OF THE HEXHAM DIVISION

May 1929

Ladies and Gentlemen, –

Eighteen months ago, I addressed three meetings, one for farmers at Hexham, and the others at Hexham and Haltwhistle, all of which I appreciated, for I greatly liked those I met. I was therefore delighted to be asked to contest the Division, and have very much enjoyed every opportunity I have had since then of getting to know the feelings and wishes of the people.

I have found everywhere a deep and growing dissatisfaction with the present Government.

Farmers have realised that the great expectations held out in Mr Baldwin's last election manifesto of restoring the great industry of Agriculture, have come to very little.

Miners feel most strongly that their industry has been badly mishandled.

Insured persons feel that they were wrongly deprived of extra benefits by the raid on their Societies' funds.

Householders and Shopkeepers feel that their claims in the matter of derating have been ignored.[1]

Women who are suffering under bad housing conditions complain that better housing seems as far as ever out of their reach.

The Tax-payers complain that expenditure has not been reduced, but increased.

Lovers of Peace are feeling ashamed that in many directions this country stands in the way of the permanent substitution of Peace for War.

And, above all, there is a deep moral indignation that the Government have drifted along for four-and-a-half years without seriously tackling the curse of Unemployment, which is steadily gnawing more deeply into the industrial life of the nation and the moral fibre of our people.

This is the feeling I have met from Falstone and Rochester to Allenheads and Blanchland, and from Gilsland and Slaggyford to Stamfordham and Wylam.

And while I have tried to understand their discontents, I have tried also to bring forward remedies for them. For as the great Statesman, Edmund Burke,[2] said a century-and a half ago, "Public Duty demands and requires that what is right should be not only made known, but made to prevail; that what is evil should not merely be detected but defeated".

The Liberal Party have in the last few years worked out detailed plans for mending what is amiss; they cover land, coal, housing, the marketing of agricultural produce, and the whole field of industry. I have taken some part in this work, and know it to be sound. The more it has been discussed and examined, the more it stands out as practical and useful.

Our land can produce more food, and support more people.

The different classes engaged in industry can be helped to work more smoothly and efficiently together for the common good.

Slums can be swept away, and new houses brought within the reach of poor people who most need them.

Evils connected with the Drink Traffic can be overcome.

Better opportunities for health can be offered to insured persons and their dependents.

Our Electoral System can be improved so as to avoid the difficulty of three-cornered contests.

In disputes between nations peaceful means of settlement can be put in the place of force, as has been done in disputes between persons.

Above all, *UNEMPLOYMENT CAN BE CONQUERED, AND IT MUST BE CONQUERED.*[3] As long as we have hundreds of thousands of families on a bare subsistence level our trade cannot recover. As long as we have useful and productive work to do, and men willing to do it, unless we give the men a chance to get on with the work we are failing to make use of our available resources. As long as we give no chance to our younger men we are wasting first-class lives.

Our plans for dealing with these questions are ready and hold the field. Both the Conservative and Labour Parties are now copying them, but if you want a thing well done it is best to give the work to those who have planned it out, and who really believe in it, and have successfully done similar work in the past. This applies to the Liberal Party only.

The Conservatives, after long neglect, are now putting forward plans similar to ours for election purposes. And most of them do not really believe in them, but in Protection, which would increase the cost of living, and decrease trade.

The Labour Party have just put forward a similar programme to ours, but most of them believe rather in nationalising all our industries, which is no solution at all of our present troubles. Divided counsels make bad work.

I ask you at the coming Election to back up those who really know their job, and can do it. I can claim to be one of them, for I have taken my share in much progressive work in the past.

We want a change: we can have a change. I ask you, by voting for me, to see that we get a change.

If you do me the honour to return me as your Member I shall serve you to the best of my ability.

Yours faithfully,

Francis D. Acland

P.S.– I shall give no written pledges, for a pledge-bound Member is a mere delegate, and useless. But I shall state my views on any political questions which you may ask me, as fully and fairly as I can.

[1.] The Rating and Valuation Act 1928 was seen as unpopular with self-employed groups like shopkeepers and small businessmen.

[2.] Edmund Burke (1729–97) was a skilled orator and a prominent member of the House of Commons from 1765 until his retirement in 1794. He is remembered for his writings on political theory including his support for the colonists in the American War of Independence and his opposition to the French Revolution.

[3.] A reference to the Liberal pamphlet of March 1929, entitled *We Can Conquer Unemployment,* which advocated a major programme of public works, particularly in areas like road and rail construction, to reduce unemployment. This commitment was the central plank of the Liberal programme in the 1929 election.

DM 1193, *The Liberal Women's News,* June 1929.

ELEANOR ACLAND TO WOMEN'S NATIONAL LIBERAL FEDERATION

June 1929

Dear Fellow Members of our Federation,

What now? That is the question, isn't it, on the lips and in the hearts of every member of this Federation of Liberal workers–at any rate in constituencies where our candidate has been defeated, and that is, alas! the great majority of constituencies. What now? Now that our high hopes have sunk low? What's the good of being a Liberal? What's the good of thinking out practical definite schemes? What's the point of having keen and able leaders and candidates, of working so doggedly, wearing ourselves out, making so many real sacrifices? It all seems to have accounted for so little amid the clash of class-warfare.

"WHAT NOW?" let us take a fair and square look at the **facts.**

Fact number one. The verdict of the Election is in the main a negative one. Roughly the votes are divided into 8 million anti-Tories. 8 million anti-Socialists. 5½ **million pro Liberals.**

This proves that 13½ million voters out of a total of 21½ millions will *not* put up with Tory-ism any more, and equally that 13½ millions are *not* willing that the operation called "Nationalisation" should be performed upon British industry. Those are two "NOTS." But something more, something positive, is proved. That is that 5½ million electors **do** want Liberalism, **do** believe in Liberalism, **do** still, despite the epidemic of class-fear and class-envy that has swept the country, upheld the old but ever young Liberal faith, that the good of the whole community comes before the good of any particular class. That is a very solid fact, all the more so when we realise, that under any fair electoral system, a party supported by 5½ million voters would be entitled to 120–130 seats in the House of Commons.

Fact number two. We actually have 59 Liberal members of Parliament. Bitterly as we deplore the defeat of many excellent candidates we can, I believe, trust the fortunate ones to present a more united front than did the Liberal Party in the last Parliament.

With leadership such as they still have under Mr. Lloyd George, Mr. Runciman, Sir Herbert Samuel, and Sir John Simon (I mention these names in alphabetical order) their decision as to how to act under very difficult circumstances will be both courageous and reasonable.

Fact number three. This small but select band of Liberals do, in theory and in fact, hold the balance. They are the only barrier left against any rash financial experiments whether Protectionist or Socialist. If they were not there in the House of Commons, one or other of the class-parties would have *carte-blanche* to do as it pleased.

"What Now?"

How came it that our hopes before the election were so out of proportion to the actual results? Of course the three-cornered business was the main factor but we knew about that beforehand and yet our hopes were high.

Did we over-estimate the rightness of our programme, the energy and agility of our leaders and candidates, the devotion of our rank and file workers? I still think not. But our estimate was wrong because, in the first place, we underestimated the forces against us. We failed to realise what must be the effect of adding to the electorate millions of new voters (both young men and women) who have never known, from personal experience, what an active Liberal Government really means and does, and who therefore for the most part think of us simply as the weakest party in the State.[1]

Secondly. We had perhaps hardly plumbed the depths of passionate resentment produced in the minds of the people by 4½ years of Tory "refusal to redress grievances" – intolerable grievances.

Those two things were outside our own control. But we were also hampered in two ways for which we, as a Party, must admit responsibility.

We were not only fighting on two flanks, but the former disunity in the Liberal ranks and the fact that only too often Liberal Members either did not vote at all or (worse still) voted in opposite lobbies, had provided our opponents with a weapon against us which both of them used constantly and greatly to our damage.

Then I think we must admit that for some time after 1924 we have been concentrating, on public platforms, too much on criticising the Conservative government; and that is a method which serves very well when there are only two parties; but when there are three parties we may thereby be making converts not only to Liberalism but to the fiercer form of anti-Toryism, namely, "Labour".

In the light of this survey let us now face our question **"What Now?"** Shall we accept the invitations so patronisingly made to us to merge with the other two parties? We cannot do so without a complete denial of our Liberal faith. It would mean declaring our belief either in Protection or in Nationalisation. Worse still it would mean abandoning our historic stand for individual Freedom. For the more one gets to know about the driving force of the Tory or the Labour party, the more one realises that neither of them really respect that freedom. We Liberals all know by sad experience something of the tyranny of the Tory Squire and the Tory employer over their cottagers and work-people. But perhaps we have not all met face to face with the equally ugly tyranny of the Labour Boss over his neighbours. The Labour Member of a Board of Guardians that grants out-door relief according to the political views of the applicants, who turns up at all Liberal meetings to watch lynx-eyed for the slightest sign of approval of what Liberal speakers are saying wields a terrible power. Personally it would go right against the grain with me to become party to the bullying methods either of the Tory or the Labour brand.

It seems to me that Liberalism must still claim our allegiance. Like Martin Luther before his Judges we must say, "Here stand I. I can do no other." If you or I or any one of us go over to other parties we should be deserting 5½ million people with whom we agree and joining people with whom we do not agree. Our work for Liberalism is not in vain although we have suffered another set back to our hopes. But we should render it vain if we now denied our faith and deserted our standards.

Eleanor Acland
President, W.N.L.F.

[1.] The Equal Franchise Act of 1928 had lowered the voting age for women from 30 to 21. Since 1910 the electorate had increased from less than 8 million to nearly 29 million. See Butler and Sloman, *British Political Facts,* p. 227.

APPENDIX 1

Parliamentary Election Results of Francis and Eleanor Acland, 1906–35

Constituency	Election	Candidate	Party	Votes	%
Richmond	1906	Francis Acland	Liberal	4,468	50.6
		Earl of Ronaldshay	Unionist	4,360	49.4
				108	1.2
Richmond	Jan 1910	W.G.A.Orde Powlett	Unionist	5,246	55.8
		Francis Acland	Liberal	4,163	44.2
				1,083	11.6
Camborne	Dec 1910	Francis Acland	Liberal	4,419	65.5
		Dr George Coates	Unionist	2,326	34.5
				2,093	31.0
Camborne	1918	Francis Acland	Liberal	7,078	52.0
		George Nicholls	Labour	6,546	48.0
				532	4.0
Tiverton	1922	H.W.S. Sparkes	Conservative	10,304	46.9
		Francis Acland	Liberal	10,230	46.5
		F. Brown	Labour	1,457	6.6
				74	0.4
Tiverton	1923 (by.)	Francis Acland	Liberal	12.041	49.9
		Gilbert Acland-Troyte	Conservative	11.638	48.1
		F. Brown	Ind. Labour	495	2.0
				403	1.8
Tiverton	1923	Francis Acland	Liberal	12,303	50.0
		Gilbert Acland-Troyte	Conservative	12,300	50.0
				3	0.0

Constituency	Election	Candidate	Party	Votes	%
Tiverton	1924	Gilbert Acland-Troyte	Conservative	13,601	53.2
		Francis Acland	Liberal	11,942	46.8
				1,659	6.4
Hexham	1929	D. Clifton Brown	Conservative	11,069	39.1
		Sir Francis Acland	Liberal	9,103	32.2
		E.O. Dunnico	Labour	8,135	28.7
				1,966	6.9
Exeter	1931	A.C. Reed	Conservative	20,360	55.2
		Lady Acland	Liberal	8,571	23.2
		J.V. Delahaye	Labour	7,958	21.6
				11,789	32.0
North Cornwall	1932 (by.)	Sir Francis Acland	Liberal	16,933	52.4
		A.M. Williams	Conservative	15,387	47.6
				1,546	4.8
North Cornwall	1935	Sir Francis Acland	Liberal	16,872	51.3
		E.R. Whitehouse	Conservative	16,036	48.7
				836	2.6

Index

Jacobs, Sam, 38
Jones, Leif, 42–3

Kearley, Sir Hudson: *see* Viscount
   Devonport
Keble College, 5
Kenworthy, Hon. Joseph Montague,
   136, 153
Kerensky, Alexander, 112
Kerry County Council, 142
Keynes, John Maynard, 15, 158, 159
Killerton, 5, 13, 15, 35, 143
Kitchener, Lord 77, 78
Knightshayes Court, 148
Koss, Stephen, 12, 29

Labour, Ministry of, 116
Labour party:
   1924 administration, 14–5, 30–1,
      146–7;
   anti-socialism, 147, 148, 155, 163,
      164, 165–6;
   appeal to radicals, 12–3, 121, 126,
      131, 134–7, 157, 158, 165;
   decline in Cornwall, 21–2, 42–3;
   female suffrage, 70, 84, 105;
   rise of socialism, 1–2, 4–5, 14, 16,
      21–6, 92, 97, 110–1, 127;
   rural position, 13–4, 18–9, 34.
   See also progressive politics
Lambert, George, 28, 29, 127, 128,
   132, 133–4
Land Inquiry Committee, 11
Land Policy, 151–3, 156, 158, 162
Lanner, 93, 95, 111
Lansdowne, 5th Marquis of, 47, 68,
   108–9
Lawrence, Susan, 116
Layland-Barratt, Sir Francis, 41
Leach, V.G., 156
League of Nations, 92, 114–5, 123,
   146
League of Young Liberals, 151
Leasehold enfranchisement, 48
Lee, Sir Arthur, 91
Liberal Imperialists, 7
Liberal party:
   1918 defeat, 13, 127, 128–9;
   1929 campaign, 4, 161–3, 164–6;
   decline, 31–2, 92, 94, 106, 121, 131,

135, 137, 148, 149, 150, 164;
fall of Asquith, 3, 12, 83–4;
female suffrage campaign, 44, 48,
   61, 65–7, 69–70, 71–2, 105;
finance, 39–40, 48, 93–4, 101, 107,
   118;
internal divisions, 17–8, 29–31, 35,
   152, 153, 154, 155–8, 160, 165;
meetings, 143, 150, 151, 152, 153,
   156;
pre-war Liberalism, 1, 6, 7, 47–56,
   60, 93;
problem of three-cornered
   contests, 27, 31–2, 162, 165.
relationship with Labour, 26–31, 44,
   125–6, 130–1;
strength in rural areas, 33–5;
See also Coalition Liberals and Free
   Liberals
Liberal & Radical Candidates Association, 159, 160–1
Liberal Summer School, 159
Liberal Unionists, 8–9
Liberal Women's Suffrage Union
   (LWSU), 3, 10, 66–7, 69–70
Lille, 76
Liskeard, 117, 118, 122
Liverpool, 138
Lloyd George, David:
   Asquith-Lloyd George split, 3, 12,
      83–4;
   attacks aristocracy, 47;
   career after 1929, 16–7, 164
   criticism of his wartime record, 25,
      102, 103, 105, 106, 109, 110, 113,
      114–5, 120–1, 122, 125–6;
   friction over General Strike, 16, 31,
      156–7, 158–61;
   land campaigns, 11, 34–5, 86–7, 90,
      152–3, 155–6, 158;
   post-war coalition, 27, 28, 29, 131,
      138, 143;
   views on female suffrage, 66;
   visits Falmouth (1910), 36;
London, 73–5, 139, 140–1, 152
London University Officers Training
   Corps, 83
Lovat, Lord, 115
Luke, William, 156
Luther, Martin, 166

Tenant farmers, 87
Thomas, C.V. 24, 41, 42, 78–9, 111
Thomas, Herbert, 37
Thorne, George, 30
Thorne, William, 152
Timber Supplies Committee, 83
Times, The, 29, 105, 115, 120
Tiverton Liberal Association, 16, 25,
    150, 152, 154, 155, 156
Tiverton (parliamentary division), 30–
    31, 37, 119, 143–50, 152, 154,
    155, 156, 167–8
Torquay (parliamentary division), 16,
    32, 54, 55
Trade unions, 22–3, 25, 42, 2–5, 111,
    116–7, 135, 138, 157
Tralee, 142
Treaty of Brest Litovsk, 113
Tregavethan, 111
Trevelyan, Sir Charles Philips, 12, 73,
    134–8
Troon, 102
Trotsky, Leon, 113, 137
Truro (town), 23
Truro Helston (parliamentary division),
    9, 55, 93
Turkey, 77, 78, 81, 112
Tyne Trade Unions conference (1919),
    135

Uglow, W.G., 42
Ulster, 9, 139–40
Unemployment, 35, 42, 51, 143–4,
    162, 163
Union of Democratic Control, 73, 104
Unionist party, 2, 6, 7, 8, 9, 39, 53, 55,
    68. *See also* Conservatives and Lib-
    eral Unionists
United Kingdom Alliance, 43

United States of America, 85, 96, 105
University of Jena, 6
Urban-rural cleavage, 33, 34, 87, 159

Vivian, John 79

Wales, 23, 33, 35, 36, 62, 63, 72, 152
Walrond, Gertrude, 6
War Office, 3, 7, 10, 56, 74, 76, 88,
    119, 123
Welsh disestablishment, 36, 51
West Briton, 4
Western Daily Mercury, 62, 70, 120
Western Morning News, 97
Westminster Gazette, 115, 142
Westmorland (parliamentary division),
    20
Whitaker's Almanac, 84–5
Whitehall, 73–5
Whitehouse, E.R., 168
Williams, A.M., 168
Williams, J.C., 38
Williams, J.F., 62, 63, 65
Wilson, Trevor, 1, 2, 28, 136, 155, 156,
    161
Wimbledon, 100
Winfrey, Sir Richard, 84, 86
Witney, 5
Women's Liberal Council, 157
Women's National Liberal Federation,
    3, 16, 17, 65–7, 71–2, 118, 142
Women's Social and Political Union
    (WSPU), 67
Worcester, 14
Workers Union, 22–3, 129

Yorkshire, 6, 111
Young, Sir Edward Hilton, 127, 128,
    131, 134

THE DEVON AND CORNWALL RECORD SOCIETY

7 The Close, Exeter EX1 1EZ

(founded 1904)

Officers (2005–6)

President:
Sir Richard Trant, KCB, DSc, DL

Chairman of Council:
Professor C.J. Holdsworth MA, PhD, FSA, FRHistS

Hon. Secretary:
Mrs E. Parkinson BSc, MA, PhD

Hon. Treasurer:
R.A. Erskine BA

Hon. Editor:
Professor A. J. Thorpe BA, PhD, FRHistS

The Devon and Cornwall Record Society promotes the study of history in the South West of England through publishing and transcribing original records. In return for the annual subscription members receive the volumes as published (normally annually) and the use of the Society's library, housed in the Westcountry Studies Library, Exeter. The library includes transcripts of parish registers relating to Devon and Cornwall as well as useful genealogical works.

Applications to join the Society or to purchase volumes should be sent to the Administrator, Devon and Cornwall Record Society, c/o The Devon and Exeter Institution, 7 The Close, Exeter EX1 1EZ.

DEVON & CORNWALL RECORD SOCIETY PUBLICATIONS

Obtainable from the Administrator, Devon and Cornwall Record Society, 7 The Close, Exeter EX1 1EZ

§ No longer available.   * Restricted availability: please enquire

ISSN/ISBN 0 901853

New Series

1§ *Devon Monastic Lands: Calendar of Particulars for Grants, 1536–1558*, ed. Joyce Youings, 1955   **04 6**

2 *Exeter in the Seventeenth Century: Tax and Rate Assessments, 1602–1699*, ed. W. G. Hoskins, 1957   **05 4**

3§ *The Diocese of Exeter in 1821: Bishop Carey's Replies to Queries before Visitation*, vol. I, Cornwall, ed. Michael Cook, 1958   **06 2**

4* *The Diocese of Exeter in 1821: Bishop Carey's Replies to Queries before Visitation*, vol. II, Devon, ed. Michael Cook, 1960   **07 0**

5§ *The Cartulary of St Michael's Mount*, ed. P. L. Hull, 1962   **08 9**

6 *The Exeter Assembly: The Minutes of the Assemblies of the United Brethren of Devon and Cornwall, 1691–1717*, as Transcribed by the Reverend Isaac Gilling, ed. Allan Brockett, 1963   **09 7**

7*, 10*, 13*, 16*, 18* *The Register of Edmund Lacy, Bishop of Exeter, 1420– 1455*. Five volumes, ed. G. R. Dunstan, 1963–1972   **10 0   12 7 15 1   02 X   17 8**

8§ *The Cartulary of Canonsleigh Abbey*, calendared & ed. Vera London, 1965   **16 X**

9§ *Benjamin Donn's Map of Devon, 1765*. Introduction by W. L. D. Ravenhill, 1965   **11 9**

11§ *Devon Inventories of the Sixteenth and Seventeenth Centuries*, ed. Margaret Cash, 1966   **13 5**

12 *Plymouth Building Accounts of the Sixteenth and Seventeenth Centuries*, ed. Edwin Welch, 1967   **14 3**

14 *The Devonshire Lay Subsidy of 1332*, ed. Audrey M. Erskine, 1969   **00 3**

15 *Churchwardens' Accounts of Ashburton, 1479–1580*, ed. Alison Hanham, 1970   **01 1**

17§ *The Caption of Seisin of the Duchy of Cornwall (1377)*, ed. P. L. Hull, 1971   **03 8**

19 *A Calendar of Cornish Glebe Terriers, 1673–1735*, ed. Richard Potts, 1974   **19 4**

20 *John Lydford's Book: the Fourteenth Century Formulary of the Archdeacon of Totnes*, ed. Dorothy M. Owen, 1975 (with Historical Manuscripts Commission) **011 440046 6**

Extra Series